PENDORA

FORGOTTEN TROLLEY PARK OF READING

BY PAUL A. DRUZBA

2015

PRINKLING PRESS

Pendora: Forgotten Trolley Park of Reading

By Paul A. Druzba

©2015 Paul A. Druzba

ISBN: 978-0-9852416-1-2

Contents

Introduction   5

History of the Trolley Park   8

The Mt. Penn Gravity   13

Neversink Mt. Railroad   17

Carsonia Park   20

Central Park   26

The Wooden Ducks   40

Miller's Family Park   43

A Baseball Field, Right?   53

Pendora's Beginnings   60

The War of the Trolley Parks   63

White City   75

Opening Day   80

Monkey See   92

1907   96

1908   105

Sham Battles   111

Cannstatter   115

Arrowsmith   124

1909   129

1910   137

1911-The Fire   138

The Reading Zoo   154

The Association   173

Real Plans   185

A Pool and Rutchie for Tillers   190

Times are Tough Again   194

Happy Days Are Here Again   197

Long Awaited Wading Pool   202

A Bangless Fourth   207

1950   218

Irma & Ruth Epler   220

Back To The Future   229

The Denglers/Omega Club   236

How Big Is Pendora Anyway?   241

Gallery   246

Concrete Stage Answer   273

Acknowledgements   274

Tying Up Loose Ends   276

Introduction

Just before the turn of the 20th Century, and prior to the advent of the automobile, most people in cities got around mainly by trolley. You took the trolley to work, and back home again. You took the trolley to go shopping, or to a doctor's appointment. For closer destinations, you walked. For much longer ones, you took the train. If you were well off financially, you had a horse and carriage, though most people didn't. But the trolley got the majority of people where they needed to go- cheaply, reliably and safely.

By the 1890's, most trolley lines were pretty well established in Reading, Pennsylvania, and wherever there were people living or working, there was a trolley line. As new neighborhoods sprang up, new trolley lines were laid to serve them. But the trolley lines did most of their business Monday through Friday.

By the early to mid-1890's, "trolley parks" began to appear all over the country. The City of Reading had several. One of the most interesting, and short-lived, was Pendora Park. If you look at Pendora today, it's hard to imagine it being anything more than a baseball field and a playground, with a stream running through it. Actually, the same could be said for Carsonia Park. Looking at it now, it's basically a housing development, with a pool and a playground by the lake. But a little more than 100 years ago, both parks were much more.

Pendora was a lavish amusement park, where thousands of people came for a day of fun. It was a place where they could go to escape the dirt and drudgery of their workaday lives. But the idea of Pendora Park was not something that appeared in a dream to someone one night. Pendora was the answer to a need in people's lives, and was the result of some earlier attempts at filling those needs.

This book is basically divided into three parts: a discussion of some other parks and attractions in the area that paved the way for Pendora; a look at the short, yet fascinating history of Pendora as an amusement park; and then an in-depth look at what has happened with Pendora in the 100 or so years since the amusement park's demise.

As always, no history is a final history. Just because I played there as a child, and just because I've spent five years or so researching Pendora Park, doesn't make me an expert on Pendora Park. There are lots of people, especially those who live or have lived in East Reading, who remember things about Pendora that I have never heard. I hope to encounter those people in the future, and I will continue to collect information and artifacts on Pendora Park, just as I continue to build my knowledge base about Neversink Mountain following my first book.

I plan to offer slide programs on Pendora, just as I do on Neversink, because it's fun, but also because it puts me into contact with people who know things about the subject that I don't yet know.

This is the first edition of this book. I'll continue adding stories, information and pictures. And when the first edition is all gone, I'll do an update, just as I did with my Neversink book.

As I mentioned in my previous book, part of my intention is to relate not just the facts of what happened, but also to put them in context of the times. In other words, to give a sense of what life was like during the time the story takes place. So in this case, I'm not just trying to relate the story of Pendora Park, but also to give readers an idea of what life was like in the late 19th and early 20th Centuries in East Reading.

In the process of research, this glimpse of the past is often found in the "trailing paragraphs" of news articles. As every journalist knows, the lead paragraphs are the ones that contain the who, what where and when. The trailing paragraphs contain the how and why. Editors are taught to cut a story's length from the bottom up, and if the editor needs to fill space the next day and doesn't cut, that's when a history researcher learns the most about what really happened, from those trailing paragraphs. That's often where you find the why and how.

It's like they say- school isn't just a place for learning- it's a place where you learn <u>how</u> to learn. And, if you're lucky, the learning continues for the rest of your life.

A Short History of Trolley Parks

Trolleys first began running in Reading in 1874, powered strictly by the horse. But horses have always been an expensive proposition, and remain so today- they must be purchased, fed, sheltered, shoed and otherwise cared-for, and if they are owned with work in mind, they must be replaced when they can no longer carry the load. Trolley companies could make money with horse-drawn trolleys, but an increase in their service area, while increasing income, would also mean an increase in costs across the board, including horses.

The situation changed in the late 1880's. Despite several years of foot dragging and indecision by City Council, a time-honored tradition in these parts, (geez, I promised myself I'd try to be nice to the City in this book)… Reading still managed to be one of the earliest cities to electrify its trolley systems, with the first electric trolley running in December of 1888.

Reading was served not by one trolley company, but by a patchwork of companies, competing with each other for territory. After all, for a trolley company to make more money, it had to increase its coverage area and ridership. And, in the trolley business, a thirst for buyouts and takeovers ensued- one that would not be rivaled again until the late 20th Century's "merger mania", which continues today.

By the 1890's, forward-thinking trolley company owners were learning that there was another way to increase ridership without increasing costs very much. The answer was the trolley park.

It's hard to pinpoint exactly where the trolley park began, most likely because it was not a sudden brainstorm, but rather an evolving process. It depends a lot on how you define the term "trolley park".

In the late 1800's, successful American cities like Reading were crowded, dirty, noisy places. The average working man (and often children) labored long hours, in jobs that left them longing for a little rest, relaxation and fun in what little free time they had. Women were no exception- working at home was a much harder job before all of today's labor-saving conveniences.

By 1890, the trolleys that people rode were powered by electricity, and trolley companies were charged a FLAT RATE for their electric consumption. Think about that for a moment- no matter how much electricity a trolley company used, they always paid the same rate. This turned out to be a pretty dumb decision on the part of electric providers like the Reading Electric Light Company- a decision for which they would pay dearly for years afterwards.

So with that in mind, the only additional costs for expanding a trolley line were for additional cars, track, maintenance and conductors. No extra horses or electricity to worry about. That's where the trolley parks came in.

Somewhere along the line (pardon the expression), someone got the idea that a good way to increase ridership (and profits) was to get people who rode the trolley during the week to also ride on weekends. But if they didn't work on weekends, where would they go?

The trolley companies needed to create a place for weary weekday workers to go on weekends. Someplace quiet, clean, safe, and fun- everything the city was not.

For a trolley company owner who was in tune with the needs of the general public, the answer was fairly simple and surprisingly cheap. Acquire some acreage outside the city, preferably wooded and beautiful, and provide a few amenities. (It's kind of like the old baseball field axiom- "If you build it, they will come").

Then, lay track from your existing line to your new destination, and suddenly your weekday riders have a good reason to ride again on weekends! Best of all, you did it without increasing your electric costs by a single Indian head penny!

To the average person in the 1890's, the idea of enjoyment was pretty simple. Clean air, clean water, (at least water that didn't stink), trees, maybe a stream or lake, and picnic tables and benches. An ice cream cone in the summer would be nice, too. My remark about the water is because many people look at the good old days through rose-colored glasses. In many ways, the good old days were certainly old, but not always good.

Anyway, this is how most trolley parks began in America, and so it was in the Reading area with the establishment of Carsonia Park in 1894. Carsonia is the best and perhaps only local example of the classic "trolley park", and most of them followed this classic formula after 1895.

But this formula took a few years to develop, and before 1895, there were some ideas being tried which would eventually lead to the establishment of trolley parks in the traditional sense. It could be said that these earlier efforts were precursors of the classic trolley park model.

The fourth model, Central Park, may be unfamiliar to you, so I'll spend a little more time on that one. I will also go into more detail on Miller's Family Park, which goes back farther than even the electrified trolley, but played a role in the development of trolley parks in the Reading, Pennsylvania area.

The Mount Penn Gravity

Tower and Hotel, Mt. Penn, Reading, Pa.

A car awaits passengers at the Tower Hotel at the peak of Mount Penn. The electrified trolley indicates the picture was from 1900 or after.

Conceived in a bar at 10th and Washington Streets in Reading in1881, the Mount Penn Gravity Railroad began chugging in 1889, (beating a competing railway on Reading's "Other" Mountain-Neversink- by a year), with a beautiful route over Mount Penn. When it started running, the Gravity had no reason in the world to stop at an ugly quarrying scar on the mountain's southern-most peak. That scar would not become the site of the

Pagoda until ten years after the Gravity was up and running.

The "Gravity" was funded not by a trolley company, but by private investors, and took advantage of pre-existing attractions on Mount Penn. Those included Mineral Spring Park, Egelman's Park, Schwartz's Summit House Hotel, The Tower Hotel, Spuhler's Mountain Resort, Kuechler's Roost Winery, Renninger's Vineyard, the Steigerwalt Winery, Miller's Family Park, the Eagle Mountain Home, and it also spawned a new attraction on Mount Penn-Wildwood Park.

There were other ways in which the Gravity did not follow the formula for trolley parks. It was powered not by electric trolleys, but by locomotives (at least at first), which pulled passenger cars to the peak of Mount Penn at the Tower Hotel (about 1200 feet above sea level). The cars were then let go, to travel back down the mountain, powered only by gravity. That made for a very quiet ride, but also one which was totally dependent upon the brakes on the car.

In the early days, the Gravity's closest connection to a trolley was its close proximity to the terminus of the East Reading Trolley system at 19th and Perkiomen, near Miller's Family Park.

But the Gravity did share some things in common with trolley parks. It was built for fun and recreation, and it did increase ridership on the city's trolley system, although the latter was not the original intention of the investors.

There were picnic facilities already established in the area at Mineral Spring Park, Egelman's, and Miller's Family Park at 19th and Forrest. But, other than the Tower Hotel, which offered dancing and bowling, the attractions on Mount Penn were mainly of the alcohol variety.

Added to this was the fun and excitement of being "let loose" at the Tower Hotel, and left to careen down the side of the mountain, by gravity, with the brakes on the car the only barrier between you and oblivion. To be honest, the fear of death is what has always made amusement park rides so much fun. Safe does not equal fun. And so, this fear must have been on the minds of many who rode on the Mount Penn Gravity Railroad.

A few times, the danger of death became more than just a possibility. One such crash occurred in August of 1890, when a Gravity car's brake failed, and the trip down the mountain became much more exciting than it was ever intended to be. The car crashed while negotiating the hairpin turn called Cemetery Curve (how appropriate), and when the dust settled, five were dead and many more injured. The official causes of the crash were listed as brake failure, and human error. There was another fatal crash a bit later.

The Gravity line became electrified (and safer) in 1898, and continued running into what was supposed to be the alcohol-free years of Prohibition in the 1920's. The railroad failed to make a profit over its last few decades, and when the tower hotel- the only significant attraction on Mount Penn- burned down in 1923, the Gravity ceased operation.

The Mount Penn Gravity did have one important thing in common with Pendora- they both increased trolley traffic, by accident.

The Neversink Mountain Railroad

Curve on Neversink Mt., near Klapperthal, Reading, Pa.

It LOOKS like a trolley, and it runs on electricity, but this is actually a railroad car, built to railroad gauge, with an electric motor, traveling on railroad gauge track. Obviously, these cars were custom built. Heading east, toward Klapperthal. The hand-colored trees are bizarre; looks like a patchwork of fall and summer.

Since Neversink was the subject of my first book, I won't go into a lot of detail that has already been covered there. For the purposes of this book, suffice it to say that the Neversink Mountain Railroad was conceived in 1889 (the year of the Gravity's opening), for much the same purpose, but for a slightly different crowd.

The Neversink was built to attract not only local patrons, as the Gravity had been, but also to give jaded visitors from Philadelphia and New York a new place to go and something fun to do. As an unexpected bonus for the Gravity, visitors from outside the area who arrived by way of the Philadelphia and Reading Railroad at the foot of Neversink, often came to enjoy rides on both mountain railways.

The view from either of these Reading mountains was likely far better than the visitors would ever encounter where they had come from. In the 1890's, meetings that were held at Klapperthal Pavilion, which was located at an actual stop on the Philadelphia and Reading Railroad, often ended with rides on first the Neversink, and then the Gravity. The two mountain railroads gave the Berks County Chamber of Commerce plenty of crow about.

The owners of the Neversink Mountain Railroad had learned a few valuable lessons from the disasters over on the Gravity, and they worked to smooth out some of the sharp curves on Neversink that might have caused problems. There was never a fatality on Neversink Mountain. The only death from the Neversink Railroad came on North 9th Street when a girl ran out in front of a car, which was traveling at a blazing six miles per hour.

The investment on Neversink (also private) included the construction of a resort hotel (the Neversink Mountain Hotel), an entertainment complex (Klapperthal Pavilion), and a beer garden adjacent to the Highland House Hotel, to attract visitors. This kind of investment was not done by the backers of the Gravity, who relied on existing attractions.

Though the Neversink Mountain Railroad operated for 27 years altogether, it was sold at auction by its original investors in 1901 after only 11 years of operation. The buyer was the Reading Traction Company, which was being run at the time by John A. Rigg. His name is important in the discussion of trolley parks, especially for his considerable efforts seven years earlier in creating Carsonia Park- the first classic trolley park in the Reading area in Pennside.

Carsonia Park

A trolley parked at the entrance to Carsonia Park, probably around 1910. The Casino can be seen on the left, and the park entrance was on the right of the picture. (Passing Scene)

If you want to be persnickety about the "classic" definition of a trolley park, and there are some who will, then Carsonia Park would be the only true example in Berks County.

Despite the fact that the additional electricity to create a trolley park was free, a chunky pile of money would still be required to create a new park from scratch.

So, with financial assistance from Philadelphia financier Robert N. Carson, John Rigg and the Reading Traction Company bought up more than 145 acres of low-lying land in Lower Alsace and Exeter Townships. For many years, this area had been known as "Custard's Bottom", named after Benjamin Custard and his wife Mary, who had settled along the Antietam Creek in the late 1700's, and who built a Georgian house that would later become the Carsonia Inn. With this land, Rigg and Carson set out creating the greatest amusement center the Reading area had ever known, or, they hoped, ever would.

In 1894, when the park opened, new track for it had just been laid from Mount Penn, down the middle of what would become a new avenue connecting Mt. Penn with the new park. Up until that point, the road that connected Mount Penn with Oley was Friedensberg Road.

Carsonia Park started out rather modestly, with picnic facilities, and not much else. More attractions were planned, but the park first needed a name.

The Reading Traction Company announced that they would entertain suggestions for a name from the students and staff of all area schools. The favorite name of the company's directors was "Lorraine Wood", and it probably would have been adopted, but there was already a park by that name in Ohio.

More than 400 names were suggested in all, and on May 21, 1896, the Reading Eagle published the list, in its entirety! The list included some real gems, including "X-Ray Park" (a little weird), "Minnihaha Park" (cute, but...), "Trolley Park" (a little too generic), "Neversink Park" (already taken, and not relevant), "Druid Park" (also a little weird), "Fairy Grove (at the time, no negative connotations), along with quite a few variations of "Rigg Park" , which today sounds kind of "crooked", as in "I think it was rigged". I wonder if the phrase came from Mr. Rigg or from another source.

Eventually, the name "Carsonia Park" was decided on, despite Mr. Rigg's claim that the name had "no special significance". The Reading Eagle would not go so far as to suggest that "money talks", but they did point out that a "Mr. Carson of Philadelphia" is one of the directors of the company. The new street from Mount Penn down to the park would become

"Carsonia Avenue", with the trolley path down the middle.

Each year after, more and more amusements and attractions would gradually be added until, just a few years after the turn of the 20th Century, Carsonia would be transforming from a "picnic park" to what we know today as an "amusement park". A few were not happy with this transformation.

In a 1909 piece published by the Reading Herald, H. A. DeForest lamented, "(In) Carsonia Park and Pendora Park ... the natural beauty has been spoiled by the erection of the gaudy devices of a pleasure park." To each his own. Money talks, and it has always been easier to make money from the thrill seeker than from the nature lover.

Competition was a major factor in the growth and development of Carsonia Park. By the end of 1905, the Klapperthal Pavilion was gone, and the Neversink Mountain Hotel had burned, so the only competition Carsonia still had over on Neversink was the Neversink Mountain Railroad, which was by then owned by Rigg. After 1901, he would have to manage it in such a way so that it wasn't TOO much competition with Carsonia. The Gravity was still around too after 1905, but nothing new was happening up there.

The natural surroundings of the park were eventually replaced with attractions like the Dodge 'Em and the "Thunderbolt" roller coaster, seen above in this 1937 photograph. (Dengler family)

Apparently, they didn't get the memo about the necessity of adding new attractions to keep customers coming. Carsonia was adding a few attractions, though slowly, because that's what visitors demanded. Then, just when it looked like they had the trolley park market all locked up for themselves, Carsonia was about to get some unwelcome competition- not in some distant part of Berks County, but right along the trolley route between Reading and Carsonia! The nerve!

Ever wondered how the trolley got its name? According to trolleystop.com, the metal wheel at the very end of the trolley pole- the part that actually touches the overhead electric wire- is called "the trolley". So, the trolley is attached to the trolley pole, which is attached to the trolley car. The result? No pollution, and very little noise other than the wheels on the track. It's ironic that most transportation vehicles since trolleys have caused lots of pollution, and much more noise. Many cities around the world, including a few in the United States, have not forgotten the logic of using trolley cars. They may be unfamiliar to you, but many thousands of people rely on them every day.

Central Park

So far, the three examples of parks/attractions that could be considered as early examples of the trolley park in the Reading area are well known. There was at least one more, and it's virtually unknown.

It all started when I was doing research for this book, and I went to visit my good friend Sandy Stief, whose family has a lot of history in the Pendora Park area. Sandy had been lucky enough to acquire a couple of very old Reading atlas books, from 1884 and 1913, and she made them available to me. They seemed to be an interesting "before and after" look at the area in East Reading where Pendora was located. A page in the atlas is like a snapshot of a given area at a particular time, including the names of the property owners, the property boundaries, the types of buildings on the property- whether they were dwellings, or barns, or ice houses, or hotels or whatever.

The atlas further describes the construction of the buildings, whether of stone or frame. It's a researcher's dream! By studying the atlas, Sandy even discovered exactly where her grandfather John Jacob Roth's house had been located in the park area.

Anyway, in perusing the 1913 atlas, I saw Pendora the way it was a couple of years after it closed, and who owned which parcels. I also saw the surrounding neighborhoods, including 18th Street and its row of homes from Perkiomen Avenue to Mineral Spring Road.

Then, we switched to the 1884 atlas. Some of the names in the Pendora area were different, including the Ice Dam, which later became the lagoon. But then my eyes wandered off to the left side of the page, and I was attracted to a big blank space, between 17th and 18th Streets, and between Haak Street and Mineral Spring Road. That's right, blank! No homes, just about five acres of open space, with only a few buildings on it, and the name of the property in big letters- Central Park.

I pointed to it, and looked at Sandy, and she shrugged. Neither one of us had ever heard of Central Park- at least not this one. Everyone knows about the Central Park in New York City, and if you do a search on it, virtually all of what you find will be about the Big Apple version. But with a little patience, one can sort out the Reading park from the New York park. OK, a LOT of patience.

In searching back for the origins of Central Park in Reading, one reaches a dead end in 1882, and nothing will be found before then, because Central

Park did not exist before 1882. The Reading Daily Times and Dispatch ran an ad in the Nov. 9, 1881 paper for the public sale of "a valuable city property."

At that time, the property contained "a two-story Swiss cottage, a barn, and tract of land, commonly known as 'Rose Valley Park'." The ad described the parcel as being in the 8th Ward, "bounded by the Mineral Spring Road on the north, 18th Street on the east, by Haak Street on the south, and by 17th Street on the west, containing five acres and 45 perches. Other than the "chalet and barn", the property was unimproved, with an abundance of trees and a "never failing spring, one square from the Perkiomen avenue Street railway, and well adapted for summer resort, school, etc."

The Rose Valley Park was purchased by Jacob S. Livengood, who set out making a few improvements to his new park. In May of 1882, he began construction of a children's playground, and the property was also re-named, and would be known hereafter as "Grand Central Park". The playground included swings, seats and benches, arbors and play houses, and a number of street lamps were ordered to light up the park.

The Swiss chalet had been known previously as "The Schweitzer House". (The German word for

Swiss is "Schweitzer"). The house was remodeled inside and out. A children's play area was added. Gas and water were introduced, new verandas built, and the house was repainted and re-papered.

The Reading Times and Dispatch article announcing the opening mentioned that a large dancing pavilion, 64 by 48 feet, had been erected on the east side of the hotel, although it shows up two years later on the atlas slightly to the north of the hotel. Attached to the dancing pavilion was a music pavilion, 20 by 30 feet, separated from the Dancing Pavilion by a railing. This entertainment building included three bars, close to the dance floor.

Easy access to alcohol was something that certainly helped to keep the Neversink and Gravity Railroads running. Perhaps they got the idea from Central Park.

This is the only known picture of the Swiss chalet, known as the Schweitzer House, later called the Central Park Hotel. The woman faces west, toward 17th Street. (Passing Scene, Vol. 3)

Meanwhile, a former Civil War Colonel named D. C. Keller was receiving an offer he couldn't refuse for "the good will and fixtures" of the St. Cloud Hotel on Penn Street above Seventh, of which he had been the proprietor. A week hence, Keller would move with his family into the "Central Park Hotel", formerly known as Rose Valley. From that moment on, both the hotel and the park went by the same name.

Like a certain Mr. Arrowsmith who would arrive on the scene about 25 years later, Col. Keller had a good sense for promotion.

The Colonel (the Civil War had only been over for 20 years, and many Civil War officers proudly retained their titles into peacetime), immediately set out constructing two ten-pin bowling alleys on the property, each four feet wide and 60 feet long.

Attached to the bowling alleys would be an anteroom with coat racks and seats for spectators. (I didn't realize that bowling could be a spectator sport. In fact, I always considered "Bowling for Dollars" on TV to be a form of torture).

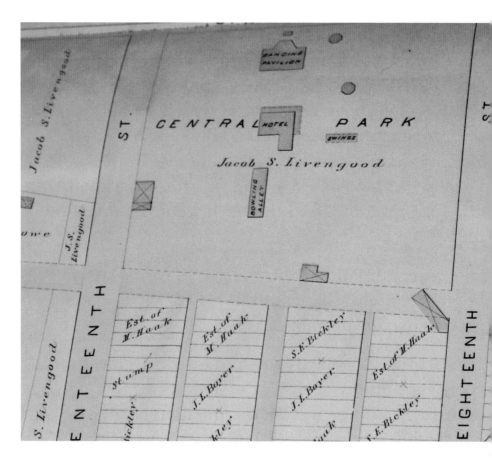

This map from the 1884 City Atlas shows Central
Park, owned by Jacob S. Livengood, with a dancing
pavilion, hotel, bowling alley, swings and a few
unnamed structures. This is the same area formerly
known as Rose Valley Park. The picture on the next
page shows what would later be Pendora Park, as it
appeared in 1884. (Sandy Stief)

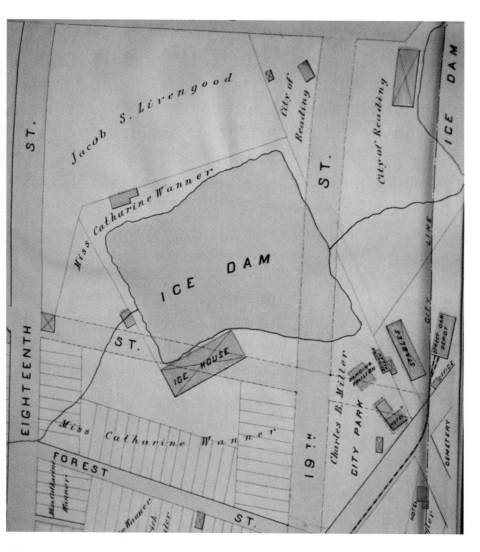

This is the 1884 view just to the right of the previous page, showing what would later become Pendora Park. At this time, Pamelia Sweney had not yet taken possession of the Pendora property, which at this point was mostly owned by Miss Catherine Wanner.

(Both maps courtesy of Sandy Stief)

Other improvements to Central Park in 1882 included a new street railway station at the beginning of the boardwalk entrance to the grounds, to accommodate people arriving or leaving the park by trolley car. The station would be fitted up as a waiting room, with a "refreshment salon for the sale of confectionery, ice cream and cakes. This station is not identified as such on the 1884 atlas, but can be seen on the southern end of the map on page 32 along Haak Street.

The trolley came out Haak Street, turned right down 18th for half a block, left onto Forrest, up Forrest to just past 19th Street, then left to the terminus, just a short walk away from the Gravity Station. There was also a new entrance gate installed at the top of Central Park, or northern end, along Mineral Spring Road.

Colonel Keller, who was 42 years old at the time, was also serving as a Berks County Commissioner. He was not the only one to see possibilities for Grand Central Park. In August, The Reading Advertising Company, an arm of the Reading Times and Dispatch, announced that they had secured the rights to sell advertising on the premises, the way billboard space is rented at sports stadiums.

The City was also considering a possible new street railway line out Mineral Spring Road, along the northern end of Keller's Central Park (the word "Grand" in the title was apparently being dropped), across the valley to Miller's Family Park, to connect with the existing tracks of the Perkiomen railway company.

Over the following year, Colonel Keller continued to make improvements to Central Park, and it became one of the premier picnic and event sites in the Reading area, pre-dating Carsonia. While Central Park was not created specifically to increase trolley ridership, it did so anyway, just as the Gravity had, and so it deserves consideration as a "trolley park".

In 1883, the Times and Dispatch reported that children of the parochial school, St. Peter's Catholic Church, were treated to a picnic at Central Park, between 400 and 500 of them. They indulged in "various amusements" throughout the day, and towards the evening there were open air sports, including a wheelbarrow race". That same article mentioned a festival taking place over at Miller's Family Park, not much more than a stone's throw away.

Hints of what was to come at Pendora were already being seen at Central Park. A "Grand Fete Champetre" August 9th featured music by the full Ringgold Band. The park was to be "lit up by thousands of lamps and lanterns", along with a "magnificent display of fireworks, worth traveling many miles to see". Entertainment at Central Park was of a "refined, attractive, varied and pleasant character, and a credit to the city." A precursor, perhaps, to a later slogan of Pendora's. Admission was 15 cents.

In April of 1884, the anniversary of the First Defenders would be celebrated by a grand banquet at Col. Keller's Central Park. Of the 105 original members who were the first to respond to President Lincoln's call for Union volunteers for the Civil War, only 42 were left, and 30 of these survivors would be present at the banquet.

The postcard view on the previous page shows the Defenders Monument, which can still be seen on Perkiomen Avenue at City Park, and was featured in the author's 2002 video on the history of Berks County, "The First 250 Years", created for the County's 250th Celebration.

As the close of the 1884 season at Central Park approached, there was another, similar reunion there, this time of the 88th Regiment of Pennsylvania Volunteers.

Colonel Keller had Central Park decked out and looking its best, with buildings decorated with flags and bunting. The Colonel also outdid himself in the preparation of the meal, which included roast turkey and duck, chicken "in every style", roast beef and many side dishes.

The regiment was known as "The Bloody 88th" because of their heavy losses in Civil War engagements. This was not only the close of the season at Central Park- it was also the close of the Colonel's proprietorship of Central Park.

On April 10, 1885, Central Park's new proprietor, John Albrecht, held a formal opening. He had long been an assistant at Bissinger's Café, and intended to put his experience to work in maintaining Central Park's reputation as one of the best patronized resorts in the Reading area.

Only a month later, there was a Charity Festival held at Central Park, in honor of the Unveiling ceremonies of the monument in Penn's Common (later City Park) of brewer Frederick Lauer, to benefit the Reading and St. Joseph's hospitals, sponsored by (no surprise) the Liquor Dealers' Association of Berks County.

Albrecht continued Keller's fine tradition of events at Central Park, as shown in the ad on the previous page, with the inclusion of a performance by Professor Stookey "on the high rope by calcium light", something which would become a regular feature in a few years at a new park just across 18th Street.

Albrecht also instituted a Thanksgiving Day target shooting competition, with turkeys, geese and ducks as prizes. "All good, bad and Sunday gunmen are invited".

I'm not sure how they got involved in the park, but in 1887, The Reading Brewing Company was to begin improvements to Central Park, including a new dancing pavilion, a new ten-pin alley, and several new summer houses.

There is a brief reference to an event taking place "near Central Park" in 1891, but nothing more is heard of the place, except a mention that the City bought the property around 1909, and later used the property for the purposes of a zoo.

Since the Zoo was located elsewhere, it can be assumed that the Central Park property was used for storage of zoo materials. The City eventually sold off the land for development, which is what happened at Carsonia Park many years later. The land became more valuable to sell for development than it was making from one 15-cent admission at a time. Central Park was short-lived, but it lasted twice as long as Pendora Park in its heyday. What's really interesting is that Pendora Park did not fall victim to the pressures toward development that had swallowed up Central Park, and much later, Carsonia Park.

The Wooden Ducks

The Wooden Ducks Association, also known at various times as the American Athletic Association, the Mt. Penn Social and Beneficial Association, and also known as the Mt. Penn Association, was a social organization of several hundred fun-loving Mt. Penn area residents who had their headquarters in the Swiss chalet of the Central Park Hotel in the 1890's.

The Association appears to have been mainly an alcohol-sodden, social bunch, and met only on Sundays at the chalet. In 1893, Joseph P. Kremp, a member, sent two live alligators from Jacksonville, Florida to the Wooden Duck Association, in what was being called "Mt. Penn Park" before the name Central Park came into use. The Wooden Ducks kept up appearances by having normal-sounding affairs at their headquarters, including a "duck supper".

The club members (well, most of them anyway), did have a good heart though. An 1894 Times article told of Jacob Reed, a 60-year old man who lived in the Rose Valley Hotel of Mount Penn Park (later the Central Hotel of Central Park).

Mr. Reed, a well-known pretzel vendor in Reading, was assaulted and robbed by two men who thought there might be money stored in the chalet.

The two thieves went to extraordinary means to gain access to the chalet, including climbing the park fence, taking an axe to the front door, and then brutally beating Mr. Reed, all for his life savings of 32 dollars.

Mr. Reed, who made his living mainly by selling pretzels and cakes at the railroad stations, had been allowed to live in the house by the Wooden Ducks, in return for "looking after the premises". He spilled out his story in German to a Times reporter who showed up before dawn at the scene of the crime. It was later discovered that one of the robbers, identified by Mr. Reed, was not only a member of the Wooden Ducks, but also a former policeman!

Later in their existence, after 1900, the Wooden Ducks began getting a reputation for being rather rowdy. The club moved from their Central Park location to a building at the corner of 18th and Haak Streets.

In a 1905 complaint against The American Athletic Association, (one of the club's various names), it was said that "the principal object of the club, also known as The Wooden Ducks, is said to be dispensing, distributing and selling drinks to its members, and providing liquor to guests."

When a special occasion called for larger social functions than the chalet could accommodate, such as a large banquet, the Wooden Ducks chose Excelsior Hall at 10th and Chestnut Streets in Reading.

In December of 1919, the Wooden Ducks' Association, one of the oldest social organizations in the city, "submitted to the call of the dry's, and gave up the ghost". After thirty years, they called it quits.

One positive thing that could be said for the Wooden Ducks was that, during their days in Central Park, some of the most important trap shooting events in the state were staged there.

Let's not be too judgmental about the Wooden Ducks Association's emphasis on alcohol though. Later, clubs like the East Ends Athletic Association were formed mainly because Pennsylvania did not allow the dispensing of alcohol in public establishments on Sundays.

Miller's Family Park

Early view of the hotel from the mid 1880's, then called "C.B. Miller's Family Park". (From the Berks History Center Library)

No doubt about it; Miller's Family Park was <u>not</u> designed to be a trolley park. That's because Charles B. Miller bought the property in 1874 for 1500 dollars, before the trolleys even ran out Perkiomen Avenue. The trolleys were still pulled by horses then, and there was nothing out that way worth sending a trolley to.

In 1874, the area between Aulenbach Cemetery and Sweney's Ice Dam was just forest, and across Perkiomen Avenue was Hiener's Wissel, a large meadow, with no signs of development yet close by. Morton Montgomery, in his 1909 "Book of Biographies", noted that "it was generally remarked that Mr. Miller had shown poor judgment in selecting a hotel so far out from the city; but our subject had his own views in the matter."

Miller did not need to be told how to run a hotel. Born in Roxborough, a suburb of Philadelphia, he had years of experience with hotels and the liquor business. He started in Gibralter, then moved to Birdsboro, then to several locations in Reading, then to Pottstown, and finally to a tract near Mount Penn Borough, still called Dengler's then.

In the early days of the Miller enterprise, he called the place "The City Park Hotel". There would have been no confusion with the City Park in Reading, because that park was still known as Penn's Common, and didn't take on the name of City Park until about 1900.

Mr. Miller must have had his own personal crystal ball, because, despite the remoteness of the property, he started building and making improvements to satisfy the crowds which he was sure would come. In 1878, he had a ten-pin bowling alley built, and a shooting gallery right next to it. A croquet ground was laid out.

In 1880, Miller was staging events that turned his Family Park into one of the most popular resorts in the area, a real destination for pleasure seekers. In August of that year, he arranged for "A grand display of Fire Works" and a balloon ascension.

Each year, the park held a special "opening" in May, recognizing that much of the business would be seasonal. And in 1885, The City Park Hotel opened to crowds now arriving by trolley out the newly established Traction Company line, which terminated practically at his door.

1500 people attended this 10th opening, and the horses "had as much as they could do to pull the cars up the heavy Penn Street grade." In a hint of things to come, the Ringgold Band boarded the cars at Second and Penn, and played along the way to Miller's establishment. There was dancing until almost midnight on the Hotel's new dancing floor.

As the years went by, the crowds grew, and it looked like Mr. Miller really did have a crystal ball. He had gambled on his Family Park, and won.

Miller continued making improvements to his park. In 1893, the large dancing pavilion was transformed into a dining room, 80 by 100 feet. The sides were closed up, and sashes containing nearly 1,000 panes of glass were installed, and the dining room would be heated by steam heat.

In 1895, he received not one, but two offers to buy his Family Park, each for $16,000 dollars. One of the offers was from a developer, who claimed he could build 48 houses on 20-foot building lots. Miller's tract was said to contain 292 feet on the old Mineral Spring Road on the east, 176 feet on Forrest Street on the south, 516 feet on Nineteenth Street on the west, and 335 feet on Park Avenue on the north. Miller refused both offers.

The Sweney Ice Dam Incident

A Brief Detour

The Sweney Ice Dam, just behind Miller's Family Park, was sometimes referred to as the Wanner Ice Dam, because Catherine Wanner had owned the lion's share of the land that the ice dam sat on. It was also known as Charlie Miller's Ice Dam, because he owned a few feet of the dam adjacent to his property. (see the map on page 35).

For many years, the lake, which was frozen in winter and the ice harvested for sale and later use, was also made available to local ice skaters. These skaters actually formed a club, the Reading Skating Society, which met and had a supply of skates stored in the Sweney Ice Dam building.

In January of 1896, the Sweneys had run several ads in the Reading Times, advertising the ice house and dam both being available for rent, which would indicate that they had acquired the ice dam land from Wanner around 1895, and didn't have a strong interest in running it.

In February, 1896, the Reading Skating Society put on their final skating carnival of the year at the ice dam, and the ice was said to have been in exceptionally fine condition. Early in April, Thomas W. Sweney, father of William P. Sweney who will figure prominently in this narrative, sold his stock of ice for the season, over 1,000 tons, to Jefferson M. Keller.

Exactly one week later, before the ice could be delivered to the buyer, there was a terrible fire at the ice house, which completely destroyed the building to the tune of $5,500, along with the entire stock of undelivered ice.

Some sparks from the ice house fire caused fires at Miller's dancing pavilion and band stand, a very short distance away. The fires at Miller's Family

Park initiated some springtime renovations for 1896, including repairs to the fire-damaged buildings, and, while Mr. Miller was at it, renovations to the hotel.

The structure was given a new paint job, an orange color, with green shutters, and many other improvements about the hotel. All 17 of the rooms in the hotel were repainted and re-papered.

Miller's Family Park Continued

By mid-1896, Charles B. Miller's health began to decline, and he transferred the Hotel and Park to his son Howard J., who was anxious to try new things. Howard had leased the Bijou saloon, 17 North 6th Street in Reading from Daniel R. Schmeck, eager to put his many years of experience working for his father to use for himself.

On Friday night, November 13th, Charles B. Miller and his son Howard sat on rocking chairs conversing at the hotel. But in the night, the elder Mr. Miller passed away. He had been suffering from Bright's disease, an ailment of the kidneys, and he was laid to rest in adjacent Aulenbach Cemetery. There is no record of the Bijou saloon after April of 1895 when Howard J. Miller took over as proprietor, but there are references to the Bijou Theatre, offering burlesque and vaudeville entertainment, which are things that Howard was very interested in.

In June of 1897, after Charles Miller's death, an ad appeared for "Keffer's Casino Theatre" in Miller's Family Park, for a performance by the Roof Garden Burlesque and Vaudeville Company, now run by Howard. It was a great deal. The admission price of only 15 cents included two car fares on the Reading and Southwestern line, and admission to the theatre! For only a nickel more, you got front row seats!

Nevertheless, only about a year and a half later, the hotel and park were transferred to Robert H. Reiff, (sometimes reported as "Reith"),who held the park's opening that June with music, this time by the full Athletic Band. Only a year later, the property was once again sold, this time by the sheriff, to Frank P. Lauer, for $12,000. Charles B. Miller would have been disappointed. Five years earlier, he could have gotten $4,000 more.

Once the Miller's Family Park property was absorbed into the new, larger amusement park, the hotel- which remained standing until 1934- became known as the Pendora Hotel, and would never again see a proprietor the likes of Charles B. Miller.

Mr. Lauer remained in possession of the hotel through the days when the Lindberg Viaduct was being built. Although some business could be had by housing some of the viaduct workers, Prohibition also took its toll. The Pendora Hotel was easy access to the city vice squads, and was repeatedly raided by city police for alcohol sales. At one point, the city threatened to shutter the place.

Mercifully, the hotel was purchased by the city for $22,500 in 1929 for "development of the Pendora Park playground." The hotel had remained in operation despite the fact that the property had been condemned for park purposes three years earlier. Ironically, the hotel was worth more in a run-down condition in 1929 than it had been in 1895 when Charles Miller was offered $16,000 for a well- kept and maintained building.

The article stated that the city was asking for estimates on a swimming pool on the property, uphill towards the swan pond. But "shortage of funds is expected to hold up the pool for at least a year." A familiar excuse for decades to come.

The hotel at Miller's Family Park, as it appeared in 1934, when it was torn down. The hotel was built in 1874 by Charles B. Miller, who also built a dance pavilion and other attractions on the property. For a while, the hotel was the regular meeting place of the Reading Press Club. In the mid 1920's, when the Lindbergh Viaduct was being built, the hotel was home to some of the workers. From 1907 on, it was known as The Pendora Hotel, and the sign can be seen on this picture. (Passing Scene)

All of the parks so far discussed played their part in setting the stage for Pendora Park. Some were early forms of a trolley park, one was a true trolley park, and Miller's and Central Park were simply resorts that found themselves adjacent to trolley lines.

I think it's important to point out something that might help to improve your understanding of early 20th Century life in Reading.

The term "resort" today usually means a hotel complex spread out over dozens, even hundreds of acres, with recreation, entertainment... a small city in itself. Around 1900, a resort was much simpler- a place where people could go for a little dancing, some food and drink, and a band concert.

Pendora Park, and Carsonia Park along with it, were something new. They began providing some of the recreation and entertainment that later resorts would feature, but without the hotel rooms or the alcohol. They became what is now known as "amusement parks". The only original trolley park in the general area that still exists today is Dorney Park in Allentown.

Pendora Park:

Just a baseball field, right?

In July of 1998, as I sat in the field house of Pendora Park, manning the history display for Pendora's part of Reading 250th Celebration, my mind raced back to my youth.

Back to 1960, when I earned a spot on the 12th and Chestnut Playground baseball team. Not that it was much of a distinction- 12th and Chestnut was probably the worst team in the playground league in Reading. It was probably much better in the early 1930's when my dad played for the team, but in the 60's, we were awful.

I remember, and sometimes still have nightmares about, a 23-0 loss to Reading Iron playground. The guys from Reading Iron were so big, it made us wonder if some Legion team had loaned players out to them. The field seemed so huge at the time, because it was really a hardball field where Legion teams played, and it seemed like a mile from home plate to first base, which I only ever reached on my way back to the outfield after three quick outs. The 12th and Chestnut team had no "field" of our own. The playground was (and remains) a small macadam lot, which at one time had been the 12th and Chestnut school.

But the good part of our 23-0 shame that day was overshadowed by one of the scariest and most-fun experiences of my young life up until that point. After our speedy loss, a couple of my teammates persuaded me to follow them through the creek tunnel, which began above the baseball field on the hill leading up to Mineral Spring Park. Rose Creek flowed into Pendora from there, and disappeared into a tunnel under the baseball field, emerging a little bit west of the field house. Despite being closed off by an iron gate, it really didn't take much for a couple of skinny kids to squeeze through.

Today's unprotected entrance to the tunnel under the baseball field. (Photo- Druzba)

On the surface, the distance covered by the tunnel is not really that far, but it seemed endless when a dumb kid was walking (stumbling) through, in almost total darkness.

I felt like a hero when I finally emerged at the other end, and my parents would never know what I was up to after the game. Yes, my clothes were wet, but they could have gotten that way in the wading pool down in the corner of the park near 18th Street. I had it all figured out.

From that day on, Pendora held a special place in my heart, and I looked forward to games on its giant baseball field, even though it usually meant another loss. I never went through the tunnel again, but it didn't matter- I could say that I did it.

About 20 years later, I would return to Pendora Park as part of a Merchants League softball team, which was a little better in the won/loss column than the 12th and Chestnut team had been. Again, I felt like I was at home every time we had a game there. So in 1998, about 20 years after the Merchants League softball games, here I was back at Pendora Park. I was a member of the Publicity Committee for the Reading 250th Celebration, and I thought it would be a kick to come up to Pendora to check out their mini festival which was part of the celebration.

When I got there, it was pretty quiet, since it was early afternoon, and most of the activities would take place later in the day. So I wandered into the field house, and I felt a chill, both physically and emotionally. It was like a flashback, but part of that was the cool comfort of the field house. It always felt that way, no matter the weather outside. It could be

100 outside, but the stone of the field house made it feel like a medieval castle.

There was a small display set up, which I volunteered to help out with- telling the story of a Pendora Park that was long gone to any visitors who stopped by. I had a few old postcards of the Pendora of ages past, but here was more history than just a few pictures could tell. I was hooked. I had to find out more.

Rosenthal

Another detour- for background information. The Rose Creek flows from Egelman's Reservoir, through the half mile (more or less) of Mineral Spring Park, and continues downhill to a flat spot that used to be called Sweney's Ice Dam. Rose Creek apparently disappears at 18th and Forrest Streets, on an underground journey beneath Perkiomen Avenue, and downhill through East Reading. The water finally emerges at South Sixth Street, where in the early 20th century Johnny Hiester's excursion boats used to take passengers on trips up and down the Schuylkill River, and empties into that river, for the final leg of its journey to the sea.

So the Rose Creek Valley (Rosenthal in the German), actually begins at Mineral Spring Park, and ends in the Schuylkill, although from an above-ground standpoint, actually ends at that 18th and Forrest Street dive underground.

It's worth noting that, in the 1960's when I had my little adventure underneath the Pendora ballfield, the entrance and exit of that portion of the creek were covered with a heavy iron barrier, which had openings large enough only to allow a skinny kid like me to wiggle through. On a photo tour in 2014, and as of this writing, I found that the iron barriers were now gone, and the only remaining barrier in sight was the one where the creek went under 18th Street at Forrest. Whose idea was it to remove the barrier above the baseball field? Did that really strike someone as a good idea? Now, in the 21st Century, I think that danger really needs to be fixed.

As far as the lower creek portion is concerned, I can't imagine anyone trying to make that underground trek from Forrest Street all the way down to South Sixth at the river, but I guess that some have done it anyway. But at least the iron barrier is there as a deterrent.

OK, enough background. Now that we've discussed the various parks and attractions in the Reading area which paved the way to the establishment of Pendora Park, it's time to move on, and tell the Pendora story.

Rose Creek says goodbye to Pendora at this 18th Street culvert, entering a tunnel that emerges at 6th Street at the Schuylkill River. This is the same type of metal barrier that used to be in place where the creek descends under the baseball field. It's obvious that the barrier can at least hold back a pillow. (Photo- Druzba)

Pendora's Beginnings

It was 1907. Teddy Roosevelt was President. The Titanic was probably still in the blueprint stage, and still four years away from sailing. In Reading, the population was exploding, from about 79,000 in 1900, to over 96,000 by 1910.

For enjoyment, folks in Reading went for a stroll or a picnic to Charles Evans Cemetery or City Park. They went down the Schuylkill on one of Captain Hiester's steamboats. And more and more, people took the trolley down to Carsonia Park, which for the past twenty years had been drawing ever-growing crowds as its attractions slowly expanded.

But none of these places changed that much, including Carsonia. Yes, they were beautiful, wooded, and a sight nicer than being in Reading, but people look for new sources of fun. And so the news in 1907 was very welcome news indeed! There was a new amusement park being planned in East Reading! True, Carsonia was east of Reading, but this new place would be IN Reading, and actually right along the trolley line that went out to Carsonia Park from downtown. It might seem odd to us now that two parks would be located in such close proximity to each other, but in 1907, it made perfect sense.

At the time, the Gravity Railroad was operating on Mount Penn, taking riders up to the summit at the tower, where they could dance, do a little bowling, and have fun before their sometimes exciting descent back down the mountain. The Gravity station was at 19th near Perkiomen. This was just a few hundred yards up the hill from Miller's Family Park.

Close by Miller's Family Park was Sweney's Ice Dam, which was basically a lake fed by the previously mentioned Rose Creek. The ice house was located roughly where the current field house is situated. In the 1890's, after harvesting ice from the lake and storing it in the ice house, the lake would often freeze again, and be opened up to ice skaters. There were actual skating clubs which used the Ice House as headquarters. This area of East Reading, in the vicinity of 19th Street, was just beginning to become a residential area around 1907.

The area surrounding Miller's had some interesting history. Captured Hessian soldiers, who were German mercenaries hired by the British to fight those ingrate rebels in Colonial America, were held encamped just above 18th Street and Mineral Spring Road. The Hessians, former enemies of the newly emerging United States, would become an important part of the German heritage of Berks County.

Later, at the start of the Civil War, Reading area volunteers, who were among the first volunteers in the country, gathered at Penn's Common, above Penn Street at 11th (now called City Park). Those first volunteers are commemorated in a monument shown on page 36.

Penn's Common soon became inadequate for the growing militia. The soldiers were soon moved to more spacious digs at Hiener's Wissel, a meadow at the foot of Neversink Mountain above 18th Street, just across Rose Valley from the Hessian Camp. Hiener's Wissel offered a small spring for drinking water. Washing required a larger flow of water, so the soldiers would take the short walk over to Rose Creek, where the water was more plentiful.

Now, in 1907, the area surrounding Rose Creek would become famous not as an encampment, but rather as a first-class amusement park- eagerly awaited by the people of Reading. But it was not so eagerly awaited by its competitors.

The War of the Trolley Parks Begins

In the spring of 1907, plans were being made for the opening of the new park. The Arrowsmith Amusement Company, headed by Arthur V. Arrowsmith, assisted by attorney Harry F. Kantner, purchased Miller's Family Park and Sweney's Ice dam early that year, from the Livingood and Sweney estates, all 14 acres of it. The charter for the new company arrived in Reading from Harrisburg on April 6, 1907. The company was capitalized for $100,000. For those not fluent in business lingo, that means they would be able to borrow $100,000 to complete the project.

The parcel purchase included land between Mineral Spring Road and Forrest Street, and between 18th Street and 19th Street. At that time, 19th Street appeared to go straight north of Perkiomen Avenue, but it was just a paper street at that point, and actually wound eastward toward Mineral Spring Park.

The outbuildings at Miller's Family Park would be dismantled by Arrowsmith, though the hotel building was left intact. A New York landscaping company was working on plans for the amusement buildings and other structures.

The old Sweney ice dam would be cleaned out, and a cement floor laid, transforming the ice dam into a lagoon. The lagoon would be surrounded by a 20-foot wide gravel walk, and an imitation marble wall. Some of the plans never went past the planning stage. For example, the dam breast was supposed to drop in stages to provide a graduated water fall, and a lily pond would be located just below. Also, a large electric tower was to be built on the other end of the lagoon, with water streaming from all corners.

The "large amphitheater" to be built around the lagoon, with a seating capacity of 2,500, was scaled down somewhat to a bandshell,

Also planned were a large dance building, 90 feet wide and 150 feet long, with an oblong ballroom equipped with sloping balconies.

The list of architect dreams included a small zoo, and the company was said to have already purchased a few animals, including two dromedaries, an elephant, and a few deer. Those would be kept in the portion of the park traditionally known as Miller's Family Park.

(The mini zoo apparently did happen, most likely the following year, in one of the amusement buildings, though it's doubtful that an elephant and camel were involved.)

Plans called for the lagoon to be drained in the fall, and the floor covered with sawdust, to accommodate football games. Apparently, the owners never considered that all of this effort would have cost serious money, and brought in no money in return.

Slides and snow chutes were also planned for winter activities and carnivals like the ones they held in Montreal. Arrowsmith did have some financial backing and high hopes, but he was not a millionaire. It was decided that Pendora would be a fair weather park, and not a year-round operation, except for the skating rink.

The list of planned buildings and attractions went on and on in this April 6, 1907 Reading Eagle story, and many never came true, including a huge building which was supposed to recreate the destruction of Pompeii.

Although it was the park's intention early on to advertise its facilities to include the Mount Penn Gravity railroad as a "great scenic railway", since it was so close by, the park instead created a miniature railway of their own by the opening date. Among the plans which <u>did</u> turn out to be true were thousands of electric lights, and frequent fireworks.

Finally, the article described plans for two entrances, one at 19th Street and Forrest, which was the main entrance, and other at the top of the 18th Street Hill at Mineral Spring Park. If the second entrance ever existed, there are no pictures or accounts of it to be found, at least at the park's opening.

Meanwhile, on Mount Penn, the operators of the Gravity, on hearing of the plans for Pendora, talked about stringing thousands of bright lights around the tower, making it visible and inviting to the people down in the city. They also talked of adding some amusement rides, including the caterpillar. If you look around the area surrounding the present day tower, there would have been plenty of room to add new attractions, although not quite as much as now. The previous tower had additional buildings housing a bowling alley and other amusements, which are now gone. The Gravity never pursued any of these attractions any farther.

These grandiose plans for Pendora also made the folks down at Carsonia, who had become rather complacent, stand up and take notice. As plans for the new amusement park in East Reading became fleshed out, efforts at Carsonia Park heated up. Carsonia's intention was to so saturate the newspapers with news about their park, that

Reading area residents would hardly notice the coming of a new one. Unfortunately for Carsonia, the folks who were planning the new park had pretty much the same idea. The resulting advertising war made the folks who sold ad space at the Reading Eagle very happy for the coming battle's contribution to their wallets. And this was not just a rattling of sabers, but rather a war which would last for at least a year.

In previous years, Carsonia Park ads would mostly be limited to very occasional small ads for special events, and not much else. But now, the paper ran splashy ads for "spectacular events in June, July and August- a series of "Children's Days" to be sponsored by the Jonathan Mould and Company store on Penn Street. The store planned to give away 75,000 children's tickets, good for free rides on the roller coaster, merry-go-round, circle swing and the Old Mill.

Each ticket was good for six rides, which was worth a total of 30 cents. That works out to a total investment of over $20,000 dollars, which in 1907 was a quite substantial sum. To the uninformed, what might have seemed like incredible generosity on the part of Mr. Mould was rather an exercise in self-interest, as Mr. Mould had a financial interest in Carsonia Park.

Yes, these Children's Days were all ready to go, except that exact dates had not been mentioned for them. The reason, according to Berks historian George M. Meiser IX, was that Carsonia did not yet know exactly when the new park in East Reading would open. When that information did become available, the Children's Days at Carsonia would be quickly scheduled to coincide with the new park's opening.

As late as May of 1907, references to the new park mainly referred to "the new amusement park." Arrowsmith still needed a name for the park, and decided on a method similar to the one that had been used to name Carsonia Park. Suggestions were invited, and 2,561 were submitted for consideration. Mercifully, this time, the entire list of entries was NOT published in the Reading paper.

The contest was won by Miss Florence E. Drase of 156 Clymer Street. "My name for your park would be Penndora Park, a corruption of Pandora, the gift of the gods, and a personification of beauty, pleasure and music." The spelling of the name also gave a nod to nearby Mount Penn.

As her reward for submitting the winning entry, Miss Drase was given 15 dollars in gold. The next-best name was "O-Go-See", a rather lame name submitted by Miss Gertrude Wolf of 619 North 9th

Street. Also, Mrs. Mary G. Bickhart of 412 North 6th Street impressed the judges with her amazingly unimaginative, yet patriotic suggestion of "Washington Park", for which she received a $2.50 gold piece. The headline in the next day's Reading Times said, "It Is Penndora Park". One of the "n's" in Penndora was soon afterward dropped by Arrowsmith, and the name became "Pendora".

All in all, the pool of names was several notches below some real gems that had been submitted ten years earlier for what became known as Carsonia Park, and the best and worst of those are noted earlier in the text.

The same article in the May 2, 1907 Reading Eagle which had announced the park naming winners, also went on to say that the new park was being graded, and a miniature railroad about a quarter of a mile long was under construction around the lagoon. All of the lumber necessary for construction was already on site for the buildings and the large fence that was planned. The work would be done as quickly as possible, to prepare Pendora Park for the planned opening on June 15th. The large columns that would grace the building facades had not yet arrived.

The June 15th date came and went, and the park was not yet ready. But Carsonia Park was doing its best to be ready for the opening of their new competitor by keeping up a steady stream of advertising.

Meanwhile, progress was being made at Pendora, but probably far too slowly for the anxious new owner. After all, it was summer- prime time for an amusement park to make money! The new amusement buildings were now under roof, although not as many as had originally been planned. The 2,250 foot midway, surrounding the lagoon, was now complete, and edged by Greek-style columns, painted white with gold trim.

Though Carsonia's ads had been increasing in frequency and size in anticipation of the opening of Pendora, they were no match for the fantastic, top half of page seven spread placed by Pendora a few days before the actual opening on July 25th, 1907, shown on the following page.

GRAND OPENING of Beautiful PENDORA PARK

Reading's Gorgeous "White City"---The New $50,000 Amusement Enterprise

THE CLEAN, REFINED FAMILY PARK FOR OUTING, RECREATION and AMUSEMENT

ALL DAY and EVENING

ALL DAY and EVENING

THURSDAY, JULY 25th

THE RINGGOLD BAND—100 Picked Musicians

The largest aggregation of musical talent ever engaged for any occasion in this city will discourse classic and popular music on the Opening Day and Evening. The rendition of the many fine selections on the programme will be, in itself, an attraction worth taking a holiday to hear.

The unveiling of this magnificent new resort—the many attractions, the surprising disclosure of beauty, grand structures, etc., will make . . .

THE OPENING DAY A MEMORABLE ONE FOR READING

—COOL and CLEAN :: RESTFUL and REFINED :: ATTRACTIVE :: ENJOYABLE—

Attractions

SHOOT THE CHUTES

SCENIC STEAM RAILWAY,
With Miniature Cars and Engine

ROLLER SKATING

PICTURE ARCADE

THEATRE,---
Spectacular Shows with fine Scenic Effects
Opening Attraction—"Pharoah's Daughter"

The Mysterious "Molly Coddle"

MUSIC ARCADE

AERIAL SWINGS

BAND CONCERTS

ORCHESTRIANS

CARROUSEL

WIRE WALKING

FIREWORKS

DANCING

RESTAURANT

SODA FOUNTAIN

ICE CREAM BOOTH

GRAND ILLUMINATIONS

Attractions

Every visitor has the freedom of the entire Park, to stroll the beautiful walks, enjoy the comfortable benches, the grand concerts, with the assurance of management's fullest consideration for their comfort and pleasure. . . . .

BEAUTIFUL PENDORA PARK

The transformation of this large section just outside the noise and heat and turmoil of our busy city into one of the most beautiful and most inviting family parks in the world will be a revelation to the people of Reading. No expense has been spared in the planning and building of this beautiful "White City."

Architecturally, the park is a dream. Pavilions, Porticyles, Arcades, Booths. Promenades, Resting Nooks, Lake and every other feature that money and skill could devise makes it the equal of any amusement park in the world.

It is a miniature "World's Fair"—a family resort, pure and simple, ideas in its constructing, attractions and management, one to which the people, young and old, will enjoy to the highest degree the satisfaction and pleasure an outing with nature and artistic surroundings can bestow. Like everyone who has seen the new amusement center, you'll pronounce "Pendora Park" with its beautiful natural advantages and its magnificent buildings, "A Garden Spot of Reading." For the mere taking of having complete control of the crowds designed to visit Pendora Park, so as to insure the best of order and greatest enjoyment for every individual, a small admission fee of 5 cents for adults will be charged. Children will be admitted free. The dozens of free privileges extended to every visitor offset the admission fee many times.

Accommodations in shady portions of the Park for Family Parties and Picnics.

Tables and benches for lunches.

GOOD WATER

ADMISSION: ADULTS, 5c; CHILDREN FREE

SCENE ALONG THE MIDWAY.

Reading Eagle photo from early July, 1907 shows the Amusement buildings mostly complete, but still pretty rough.

Over the next four years, Carsonia would answer not only the newspaper ads that Pendora would place, but also play a game of "keep up with the Joneses", matching Pendora's attractions, tit for tat. As for the miniature railway at Pendora, the folks at Carsonia watched with interest, waiting to see if the expensive attraction would be a winner.

MERRY-GO-ROUND AT THE LAKE SIDE. .

Pre-opening Eagle photo shows the carousel building complete. The view of Mount Penn in the background to the right would be graced by the Lindberg Viaduct 20 years later. These pre-opening pictures are not the greatest quality, because they're copied from old newspaper article microfilm. Still, they are unique, and early photos of Pendora Park are like hen's teeth. I did the best with these that I could.

GLIMPSE DOWN THE SHOOT-THE-CHUTES—MERRY-GO-ROUND IN THE DISTANCE.

The last of the pre-opening Eagle photos shows a rare view from above the Shoot the Chutes, looking down on the lagoon and the Carousel. Unlike most of today's flume rides, which fall into water that's about two feet deep, the Shoot the Chutes descended into water that was four feet deep at that point in the lake. It's amazing how few early photos exist of Pendora Park. I'm betting there are some salted away in old family albums.

White City

Much of the advertising for Pendora Park centered on the concept of the "White City". This had become a popular name for a good number of public attractions at the time, in an effort to emphasize how clean they were. All woodwork was painted white, and newfangled electric lights were placed everywhere, for a clean look in daylight, and a dazzling look at night. This concept can still be seen in action at many of today's amusement parks.

The first reference to a "white city" that I've come across was in connection with the Columbian Exposition of 1892-3 in Chicago. Although the Chicago Expo would have swallowed Pendora, the parallels between the two are striking. Not only did both refer to themselves as The White City, but both were also built around a lagoon. The White City theme continued at the St. Louis World's Fair in 1904. Another lagoon-turned World's Fair occurred in 1964 in New York, which I was lucky enough to attend.

Today, World's Fairs are a thing of the past, having been replaced by Disney World. It's funny- countries will not spend money on an exhibit at a one-year-plus World's Fair, but they don't mind shelling out billions on the Olympics, which only last for a few weeks.

A postcard from the 1893 Columbian Exposition in Chicago.

This five-pound book on the Columbian Exposition was printed in Reading in 1893, and could have served as inspiration for Mr. Arrowsmith in designing Pendora Park. (Druzba)

The Columbian Exposition also did one more very important thing- it established the amusement park as an American institution, introducing the ferris wheel, and the amusement midway.

The white city was a reaction to the fact that big cities were dirty places, and after a week of getting dirty, people were looking for places of beauty to take their families- places that were, above all, clean. A woman of that time knew that, in order to get her husband's shirts really clean, they were stretched out in the out of doors after laundering, and left in the sunshine for hours, to bleach them as white as possible. Suddenly, the electric lights began appearing over at Carsonia Park, and their maintenance people started buying up quantities of white paint.

By the way, around that time, people who did not have enough of a back yard to lay out their clothing to bleach in the sun would take their laundry up to City Park, where there was plenty of room to spread out the shirts. Now that the sheep had been kicked out of City Park, it was a much cleaner place too.

PENDORA PARK BY NIGHT, READING, PA.

Thousands of electric lights create a dazzling sight reflected off the lagoon at Pendora Park in this postcard scene from around 1908. The Amusement building stands tall among the row of attractions. In the distance over on the left, a point of light near the peak of the hill locates the Highland House Hotel over on Neversink Mountain. The Neversink Mountain Hotel, which would have been behind the trees on the left, burned about three years previous. The lagoon shown would be approximately at the site of the present-day baseball field at Pendora. (Druzba)

Opening Day, July 25, 1907

Much to the chagrin of the folks over at Carsonia Park, opening day at Pendora, though it was about six weeks late of original estimates, was a smashing success. Attendance at Pendora that day was estimated at 20,000, which is even more amazing when you consider that opening day was a Thursday.

Opening day festivities included a parade up Penn Street and out to the park (quite a trek) by the ever-popular Ringgold Band. On the way along the roughly two mile route, beginning at Third and Penn Streets around 7:15 p.m., up to Perkiomen Avenue and out to the park. It was the largest Ringgold Band that had been seen here in a while, 100 members in all, and the first piece the band played on the trip to the park was "The Pendora March", which had been specially penned by director Monroe A. Althouse for the occasion. The piece was once again played as the band entered the park. Once in the park, the Ringgold band took up position in the bandshell, and played encores all evening.

"James Bard, the senior member of the famous "Bard Brothers" team of acrobats, and slack and tight-wire performers, gave an exhibition of wire walking." It was undoubtedly a sight never seen by virtually everyone in attendance. "At a prearranged signal, Mr. Bard set off a set piece of fireworks that was suspended from the tight wire over the center of the lake. A glimpse of the performer could be seen through the blaze of rockets and redlights as he stood on the wire in the center of the piece. The act was greeted with prolonged applause. At the conclusion of this daring feat, there was a splendid display of fireworks from the pier at the north shore of the lake."

After the opening day festivities, owner Arthur Arrowsmith said, "I am glad everybody seems pleased with Pendora. Many finishing touches must yet be given, and from now on, details shall receive more attention. The park will be made much prettier... It is certainly gratifying- such appreciation of my efforts in launching the new enterprise, and I will give best of all evidence of this appreciation, by giving clean amusement, and managing Pendora as a first class refined resort, equal to any in the land. I also wish to say that Pendora will positively not be open Sundays. It will be operated 6 days a week only." This statement made it sound as if it were a personal conviction instead of a legal requirement. It's unclear which it actually was.

In 2014, I spoke with the Ringgold Band's current director, Jim Seidel, about the Pendora March. My understanding is that the Ringgold Band quarters suffered a fire in the 20th Century which destroyed a lot of the sheet music that was stored there, and that the Pendora March was one piece which did not survive. Mr. Seidel said that he had never seen it, but promised that if it ever turned up, he would let me know. Stay tuned. Perhaps a 1907 band member kept a copy.

On opening day, visitors entered Pendora at the main gate, at 19th and Forest Streets, just off Perkiomen Avenue. And there was plenty of fun in store for those visitors.

People came from all over the city, and every trolley car headed for East Reading was "crowded to its utmost capacity", while the thousands who lived close to the park simply walked there.

The Reading Eagle reported that "the entrance on Nineteenth Street was crowded all evening, and ticket sellers and takers were kept busy. The east end of the park takes in the grove formerly known as Miller's family park, and visitors were surprised at the remarkable transformation. Benches and tables for pic-nickers, swings and other forms of amusement are scattered throughout the grove." No mention of the supposed entrance at 18th and Mineral Spring Road.

"What was once the old Sweney ice dam is not one of the prettiest lakes imaginable. The fact that it is not an artificial lake, but has been there as far back as the oldest citizens of this section can remember, is a feature worth considering."

The article continued by describing the pathway that lined the shore of the lake, "through the Plaza, as the thoroughfare at the western end of the lagoon is known, and over the boardwalk, which is at the eastern end of the lake, are strings of electric bulbs."

The boardwalk in front of the bandstand contained benches, so that visitors could sit and enjoy the music up close. On the northern end of the lake, next to where the Shoot The Chutes was located, was a platform that extended into the water, and it was from here that fireworks were launched. According to the article, the carousel was not yet in operation for the park's opening.

Pendora admission was five cents for adults, and free for children. Visitors were lured by attractions like the Shoot the Chutes, very similar to the present day Log Flume rides at various parks. Riders boarded a wooden vehicle, which was pulled up a ramp high above the lagoon, and then released to slide down the greased, wooden boards of the ramp, only contacting water when it splashed into the lagoon below. No doubt the riders were screaming their heads off all the way down. Nowadays, we know what to expect on log flume rides. But in those days, the Shoot the Chutes was a brand new thing, and much more scary (fun).

The Shoot the Chutes ramp had two channels for boats, and there were ten boats altogether, with seating capacities from six to ten per boat. The descending boats could not be seen from below until they were about halfway down, and they landed in water that was about four feet deep at that spot.

There were eight amusement buildings, instead of the originally planned 15. The main structure, on the left as you looked from out on the lagoon, turned out NOT to be mirrored by another similar building to the right. The building served as an amphitheater, and housed a roller skating rink with organ.

The smaller amusement buildings were occupied by an ice cream parlor, penny arcades and other attractions. A bowling alley and some other attractions were built along the hillside next to the dam breast for the lagoon. On the extreme eastern end of the park, along Forrest Street, there were lots of trees and picnic facilities. A dozen swings had already been set up, with "automatic brakes to stop them at will", and more were planned.

Two carloads of sand were on order, to be placed in this area for the children.

Pavilions were planned along the hillside on the west end (18th Street), for private picnic parties. Two officers would be stationed at the park to keep order. No pictures exist of a large "reception room for women", which would include washstands, towels, and "a colored woman in attendance".

On opening day, visitors could view a newfangled motion picture called "The Pharoah's Daughter", which would keep viewers spellbound for about 30 minutes.

The most sought-after bands in the area, including a specially-selected Ringgold Band of 100 pieces, performed in the park's bandshell. Visitors could be thrilled riding the aerial swings, be dazzled by aerial wire walkers tip-toeing above the lagoon, enjoy a restaurant and soda fountain, and much more. You got a lot for your nickel admission.

Reading, Pa.   The entrance, Pendora Park.

One of the entrances to Pendora Park. Please look carefully at the people, and then look at the picture on the next page.

ENTRANCE TO PENDORA PARK, READING, PA.

This is the same picture as the last one, but the postcard artist added more spectators on the previous version. 100 years before Photoshop! (Druzba)

All of the electric lights at Pendora also inspired the nickname "The Luna Park of Reading", which would be seen on subsequent ads. Pendora flattered itself to suggest comparison to the much larger Luna Park of Coney Island in New York. Luna Park in New York was never really a park, but rather "a neighborhood in Brooklyn that featured a collection of amusements, including several independent amusement parks," according to Jim Futrell, in his book "Amusement Parks of Pennsylvania".

Visitors to Pendora could also ride a miniature railway, a quarter of a mile journey around the lagoon, which would have been especially beautiful at night. You could ride the carousel or the aerial swings, enjoy dancing and fireworks, and go roller skating indoors to organ music. Outside of opening day, the names of the movies being shown were never advertised in those days, most likely because the movie-making craft was brand new, and there wasn't yet much to see! And since most people had never seen a movie before, it really didn't matter what the subject was anyway.

A postcard showing the Amusement Building in center, with the skating rink and the end of the railway on the left. (Druzba)

While many attractions at Pendora each cost a nickel, there was also a five-cent admission charge. That was because some people came to Pendora just to picnic, and the 5-cent admission got them into a lush, wooden picnic area, where they could unpack their lunch, and enjoy the sights and sounds of a park full of fun, all for just a nickel. Even with only a five-cent admission charge to the park, the owners took in close to $1,000 just in admission fees, not counting what was collected for various rides and amusements.

This real photo postcard shows a unique view of the amusement area at Pendora. Real photo postcards like this were different from the usual lithograph postcards. Although all postcards originated as photographs, lithographs were hand-colored, and often "doctored" to include people who were not in the picture originally. The above photo was probably taken on a Sunday, when the park was closed. Note the railroad tracks in the foreground. (Druzba)

Considering that the park cost $50,000 to build, the first day's take was seen as a great beginning. $50,000 could not build a home today, but in 1907, it could build a palace. And with a great start like opening day at Pendora, the owners could expect a good return on their investment. As long as every day was as good as opening day.

A boat splashes down on the Shoot the Chutes ride. A sharp eye (and maybe a magnifying glass) can see a horse and buggy approaching the ramp on the left. (Druzba)

Monkey See...

Pendora's opening day take was not lost on the owners of Carsonia Park. And neither were the new attractions. Almost immediately, Carsonia got to work on its own version of the Shoot the Chutes, which was enormously popular over at Pendora. Carsonia also began to bring in high-wire acts, and installed a skating rink. They even went so far as to install white-painted columns around their lake. Carsonia would soon begin to resemble Pendora Park east, and they were definitely on the defensive.

In the case of Carsonia Park, imitation wasn't meant as flattery, as the old saying would suggest, but rather as a return volley. The American Amusement Company, which had taken over operations of Carsonia from the United Traction Company a few years earlier, made sure their Shoot the Chutes was bigger, and was bathed in bright lights. In fact, just after Pendora's opening, the Carsonia operators noted that they had "just purchased" several thousand colored incandescent lights, which would form a "Fairy Walk" from the trolley depot to the theatre at Carsonia.

Carsonia's Shoot the Chutes appeared only a few months after Pendora's. By the 1920's, it was removed to make room for the swimming pool. (Passing Scene)

The Carsonia operators made it sound as though they were planning to do all of this anyway, regardless of what Pendora turned out like. In fact, Carsonia's decision about lighting was to counter Pendora's claim that there would not be a dark spot in the park, with bright lights everywhere.

Carsonia also began work on an indoor roller skating rink, set to open the following season in 1908, to rival the one at Pendora. Even the existing buildings at Carsonia were painted white, as well as the benches surrounding the lake. Carsonia began to resemble another "White City".

And, near the end of the 1907 season, Carsonia announced that it would invest $18,000 in a miniature railway to circumnavigate the lake in 1908. The obsession with imitation and promotional budget for 1907 was very costly to the operators of Carsonia Park. The tit for tat was also very costly to the Arrowsmith Amusement Company, and the effects were starting to take their toll by the end of Pendora's first season.

But it took a little while for caution to take root in Mr. Arrowsmith. Only a few weeks after the opening of Pendora, he purchased a new ride called the Ocean Wave. It was set up in the park's plaza, and the ride's advertising promised it would be a fantastic money maker. Don't they all?

Mr. Arrowsmith was no doubt influenced by an ad just like this, which appeared in 1907, promoting a new amusement ride which had just been developed and patented by the Armitage and Guinn Company. After only two months, Arrowsmith realized that he would probably never recoup the money he spent on this attraction. Regardless of the selling price of the ride, making $450 in one day at a nickel per rider would mean 9,000 riders a day)

(Courtesy of Jim Abbate, of the National Amusement Park Historical Assocation)

95

1907

Throughout the 1907 season, Pendora Park continued to maintain their aggressiveness in promoting the park and keeping up with the changing tastes of customers. They continued to hire aerial acts, which is something that had become one of the park's hallmarks in their opening season. In July, an ad mentioned the "Happy Hooligan", who would "risk his life tonight on the 3/8 inch wire 75 feet above the waters of the lagoon. This is the funniest of aerialist Bard's acts".

On that night, the "Molly Coddle" opened- "a continuous round of sensational surprises from the scenes reproduced from the famous Café del Monte in Paris, to the "Hump the Hump" or "23rd Staircase Degree".

The ad also teased ahead to a new ride- "The Ocean Wave"- Pendora's own name for the "Circling Wave" device just introduced by the Armitage and Guinn company of Springville, New York. The ad touted the ride as "the greatest amusement of the day- which was now being erected in the plaza".

Finally, the ad looked ahead to the following night, August 1st, when the great "Velmont" would put his life at risk, by diving into four feet of water from a height of 80 feet, and the surface of the water would be on fire to boot! Velmont's own body would be a flaming comet! People were still holding their outings at Pendora that summer. On August 4th, a "delightful time was spent at Pendora Park" by a party including Mrs. Charles B. Miller, whose late husband had conducted the resort which was known at Miller's Family Park.

Although Arrowsmith still owned the business and made all the decisions about which attractions to add or subtract, he was not the day to day manager of Pendora. That honor fell to Elmer E. Rutter, who for eight years had been the Assistant Manager and Treasurer of the Academy of Music in Reading. Rutter had been offered positions to manage theatres in a number of cities, but preferred to remain with his family in Reading.

Ribble and Hess, the Great Roman and Spanish Ring Act gymnastic stars, continued to be a favorite attraction at Pendora in 1907, with their "fine performances of skill and strength". They were booked to appear on the Open Stage on the north side of the lagoon, near the Bandshell, so that everyone in the park could see their act.

Another popular attraction in amusement parks in those days, and in Pendora as well, was a theatre in which stories were illustrated. On August 7th, Pendora's "Bijou Dream" theatre was featuring "Fire

Boats on the Deleware (sic)" among other presentations. The Ocean Wave was under construction for over a week, and was due to be ready soon. Time was of the essence in a place like Pendora, because the season was short, and would be over by the end of September. So every day that an attraction was not available was lost revenue. Of course, Carsonia Park was under the same seasonal time constraints, but Pendora was only open six days a week.

Arrowsmith was adamant about never being open on a Sunday. It's not clear whether this was a religious conviction, or related to an early law which prevented certain amusements from being presented on Sundays in Reading. That law would not have applied to Carsonia, which was outside the city limits.

Meanwhile, over at Carsonia, arrangements were being completed to create a 20-foot wide walk around the lake, a "Lover's Lane"- much like the one over at Pendora. Trolleys were bringing loads of gravel screenings to Carsonia for the walkway, in the same way that they would later bring down cinders from the electric power plants, to fill in parts of the lake for the construction of the housing project which began when Carsonia closed in 1950.

Ads for Carsonia Park continued throughout the season of 1907, promising bigger and better attractions in the coming year. Meanwhile, ads for Pendora were becoming smaller, and promising less for the future. It seemed that the cost of keeping up with Carsonia was taking its toll on Mr. Arrowsmith.

In December of 1907, a few months after both parks had closed for the season, an ad appeared, offering for sale both the Hershell-Spillman Company Merry-Go-Round, which had barely begun operation at Pendora, and the Armitage & Guinn "Ocean Wave", "both in good condition." Prospective buyers could contact the Arrowsmith Amusement Company at Pandora (sic) Park, Reading, PA. Pendora Park continues to be misspelled to this day. Try Googling Pendora, and see what happens.

FOR SALE!
A HERSHELL-SPILLMAN CO.
Merry-Go-Round
AND AN ARMITAGE & GUINN
Ocean Wave
Both in Good Condition.
ARROWSMITH AMUSEMENT CO.,
Pandora Park, Reading, Pa.

Note: When one considers the attractions at the new Pendora Park, it's important to compare apples to apples. I don't mean to apologize for Pendora Park, but, while Pendora did not have a roller coaster, or

The Old Mill, or the Cuddle Up in 1907, Carsonia did not have any of those features until decades later. In 1907, Carsonia was still a pretty basic park, with few "amusements", and so they both grew into "amusement parks" together.

This old postcard view, from around 1907, shows an unusual view of the lake looking northwest. Present day perspective would be looking in toward home plate from right field. What is most unusual about the view is the stand mounted atop the pole on the left side- for the trapeze artists. The trapeze wires can be seen along the upper third of the view, leading to another similar stand on the other side of the lake near the Shoot the Chutes ride. Unlike most Pendora Park postcards, this view was not altered to show lots of well-dressed visitors. Again, probably photographed on a Sunday. (Druzba)

The Miniature Railway at Pendora, parked on the east side of the lagoon, between the Carousel and the Bandshell. The Amusement Buildings and the Butt House (more on that later) can be seen in the background. Pendora Park featured the railway on opening day, and Carsonia followed with their own $18,000 version a year later. Note: Whether the $18,000 figure was an actual expenditure or just braggadocio on the part of Carsonia, it would be $450,000 in today's money. This was big business!

(Photo courtesy of George M. Meiser IX, from the Historical Review of Berks County)

Reading, Pa.   Band Pavilion and Shoot the Chutes, Pendora Park.

This postcard view shows an unusually quiet moment at Pendora, with only a few Victorian strollers, who may or may not have existed. Note the admission ticket kiosk at the Shoot the Chutes ride, and also the platform to the left of the ride, where fireworks were set off. This set of color postcards were probably made at the park's opening in 1907. There were about a dozen altogether, and no other sets were ever made as far as I know. In the trees to the left of the bandshell is the Hartman home, which first noticed the fire in 1911. (From the author's personal collection)

BAND PAVILLION PENDORA PARK, READING, PA.

This postcard view, taken from a more westerly vantage point, shows the bandshell and the Shoot the Chutes Ride, and a more complete view of the fireworks platform. You can also see on the extreme left a ladder which seems to go up to nowhere. This is one of the ladders that was used as access to the high wire above the lake. Today, the Lindberg Viaduct would be visible behind the bandshell. Keep in mind that the Shoot the Chutes ride was twice as long as it appears in this picture. Only half could be seen below the trees.

This view shows the approximate location of the Bandshell, which would have been just off the right half of this view, and the Shoot the Chutes, which would have come down from the hill on the left. In the days of the Pendora Amusement Park, the baseball players shown would have been up to their waist in water from the lagoon. The section where the viaduct shows through would have originally been wooded. Photo- Druzba)

1908

Pendora Park's second season opened on a very odd, and perhaps telling note. Just as they had in their inaugural season, Pendora decided to again open on a Thursday, May 28th, 1908. Carsonia Park's opening date was Saturday, May 30th. But on Monday, May 25th, the Reading Eagle reported that thousands of people had taken the trolley to Carsonia Park on Sunday, May 24th.

This seems odd, because thousands of people found enough reason to visit Carsonia Park on Sunday the 24th, although that park was not technically "open" yet. There must have been something going on there to draw thousands of people.

It's also telling, because thousands of people did NOT find a reason to go to Pendora Park on Sunday, the 24th, because Pendora was closed on that and every Sunday. From Mr. Arrowsmith's comments on opening day in 1907, the decision to stay closed on Sundays seemed to be his idea. But the thousands of people who took the trolley to Carsonia on the 24th had no problem with a Sunday in the park. This is especially important when you consider that the operating season was so short for both parks- only about 120 days a year. By making his decision to stay closed on Sundays, Mr.

Arrowsmith shortened his operating season by an additional 16 days a year.

After the end of the 1907 season, Arrowsmith had offered up the park's carousel and Ocean Wave ride for sale. A similar ad appeared again in April, 1908. Judging by Pendora's big ad in the May 25th, 1908 Reading Eagle announcing the park's 1908 opening on the 28th, the sale of the Ocean Wave and the carousel had apparently been successful.

Opening day on May 28 began much the same as the previous year's had begun- with a parade up Penn Street, once again starting at Third and Penn. This time, there were THREE smaller bands in the parade instead of one big one. The Philharmonic Band, consisting of 23 men in red uniforms, followed by the 25 white-clad men of the Ringgold Band, followed by the 25 men of the Colonial Band in, of course, blue uniforms. The bands took turns playing. (Thank God- there is nothing worse than two or three marching bands playing at once!) The stars of the new season's shows were all in attendance, including the Aerial Lloyds, Florence Austin of the shooting gallery, Irene Ritter, the theatre's pianist, and even Evelyn Navlilus, singer in the Bijou Dream.

There is no mention of "The Pendora March" being reprised for 1908. At the head of the parade was a platoon of seven policemen, followed by a barouche (a four-wheeled carriage pulled by horses). The carriage contained Mr. Arrowsmith and his daughter Helen, and William Sweney (son of the park's former landowner).

Although there were three bands in the parade, upon reaching the park, the Ringgold Band set up in the bandshell, and played the Star Spangled Banner, while Miss Arrowsmith "raised the flag to a shower of redfire and rockets".

The Colonial Band treated skaters to music in the skating rink, with some of the band members positioned on an elevated platform above the rink, and the rest down below. The Philharmonic Band performed in the Indian Village. (Where did the Indian Village come from? Actually, it wasn't finished yet, because the Indian troupe had yet to arrive. Between the new refreshment stand and the bandshell was to be a new restaurant, not yet completed, followed by the new mini-zoo, with its monkeys, tropical birds and bears. Of course, the ever popular Shoot the Chutes were running full time. So was the little engine of the miniature railway.

Also, a small portion of the lagoon where the Rose Creek emptied into it had been filled in, to provide more seating for those who wished to enjoy the music in the bandshell. It's mind-boggling to think what all this must have cost Arrowsmith.

At 9:45 p.m., the Aerial Lloyds performed hair-raising stunts from the floating platform, followed by a spectacular fireworks display.

All of the attendants on opening day were decked out in white yachting costumes, with caps that said "Pendora" in gold letters. Oh, to have one of those caps now!

Arrowsmith sounded upbeat about the coming season. Although he had been keeping the park's improvements under wraps, he was more open as the season open approached.

The aforementioned "miniature menagerie" included bears, monkeys, tropical birds and other animals purchased from a New York farm. (There was no mention of where this "menagerie" was located, but judging by the promises before the 1907 opening, the location then was supposed to be over toward Miller's Family Park. A fleet of white swans had also been placed on the lagoon, and a school of beautiful gold fish placed in it.

The addition to the inlet was a floating stage, upon which "up to date acts will be presented." (Presumably, the "inlet" was the spot where Rose

Creek emptied into the lagoon- just downhill from where it now goes underground).

Other improvements at Pendora included improved electric lighting- 5,000 more bulbs so "there will not be a dark spot in the park." The electric effects of these lights were to be changed each week.

As one entered the park and approached the midway, the first new attraction to be seen would be the Temple of Refreshments, a rather overblown description of a refreshment stand, which now stood in the building formerly occupied by the carousel. The plaza now featured a rifle range, in the charge of Miss Florence Austin, champion female sharpshooter, who would be doing fancy shooting every day.

Next to the shooting range would be the "House of Monomania", a curious name for a fun house that either complemented or replaced the Molly Coddle. Keep walking, and you would encounter the "Hall of Vaudeville", where thrilling illusions would compete with vaudeville acts. The Bijou Dream would continue its high grade of pictures.

Pendora's popular skating rink had been enlarged, with the addition of 50 more feet of skating space now stretching the rink from the water fall of the dam breast, to the refreshment booth. The skating floor was freshly planed, and a new stock of skates had been purchased.

And what about the carousel which had been sold off before the 1908 season? It had been replaced by a new, $20,000 Carrousel (sic), with a $5.000 pipe organ! The new carousel, built by Gustave Dentzel, was located just east of the site of the old one, where the Ocean Wave had been, and was "one of the finest ever seen about here". It boasted 36 galloping figures, along with what were being called "benzene buggies"- representations of automobiles.

One thing that was NOT being changed at Pendora Park in 1908, was the fact that the park would continue to be NOT open on Sundays. Possibly related to the Sunday prohibition, was the new Pendora motto: "Fun Without Vulgarity".

Meanwhile, over in Pennside, Carsonia was also touting its improvements for 1908. These included a big scenic railway, a "trip to the North Pole", a new mammoth roller rink, a new bandshell and open air theatre, and other improvements, totaling "$45,000". So, the big question seemed to be, who could spend more money?

Trip to North Pole & Circle Swing, Carsonia Park
READING, PA.

Carsonia Park had plenty of room, not only geographically, but also financially, to add attractions like this in 1908.

Sham Battles

In the summer of 1908, the carnage of World War I, "The Great War", was still nine years in the future. And the Spanish American War at the end of the last century had seemed nothing more than a boyish adventure. And so, in this peaceful time, war games were something that many boys, young and old, were drawn to.

Arrowsmith did not have the cash to keep up with the Carsonia Park people, but he did have a good imagination. So he tended to put on exhibitions and programs that were showy, but not very expensive. Sham battles fell into that category very nicely.

During the month of August, Pendora put on three sham battles, which were very similar to today's re-enactments, although these sham battles did not seek to recall any particular war, since most of the audience would have no memory of any meaningful conflict since the Civil War, and they could only recall dusty stories told by their fathers, or grandfathers.

So several dozen re-enactors, divided between the Blue and Brown sides, would follow a prescribed plan of attack, and then victory or defeat, to the delight of thousands of visitors.

On one particular night, August 17th, the battle began promptly at 9 p.m., as the Browns, commanded by Lieutenant Ramsey, left camp and made a forced march across the park. Captain Jones, who was in command of the Blues, resisted the attack of the Browns, and drew the Brown forces into the woods, forcing their surrender. Total time of the battle- 22 minutes. That was brief enough that it would not bore even today's youth with their short attention spans.

These battles were very popular with the public, and judging by the newspaper ads at the time, were more exciting than anything going on over at Carsonia just then. Beneath or next to the Pendora ads or pictures of the battles, all Carsonia could manage was a small ad for their newly enlarged roller skating rink (see ad next page). Pendora had enlarged its rink also, but Carsonia called theirs "The Mammoth Rink". It appeared to be turning into a war of adjectives.

But the sparring continued. Carsonia's roller rink ad would mention skating music in the afternoon and evening, where Pendora only offered music in the evening. Never mind that most skaters came out in the evening, and there were relatively few afternoon skaters, which is why Pendora didn't offer music then. And the Eagle encouraged the competition, by placing the ads adjacent to each other. The war of the parks continued, but Pendora seemed to be in retreat.

SHAM BATTLE and INSPECTION TONIGHT at PENDORA

CONTINUOUS MUSIC AT THE RINK AFTER 9 O'CLOCK EVERY EVENING

like the soldier life and expect to have a pleasant experience during their three-year term of enlistment.

William H. Bitler and Isaac E. Kulp, of town, who were visiting friends at York, returned home.

A cottage prayer meeting was held at the residence of William Maxton, near Kulptown, on Thursday evening by some of the members of

114

Cannstatter

Arthur V. Arrowsmith, the President of Arrowsmith Amusement Company, may not have been a rich man, but he was a smart one, and was good at promotion. Although some eastern and southern European immigrants were beginning to arrive in Reading, including my grandfather Anthony in 1911, most of the people around here were of German ancestry.

And so, to appeal to those of German descent, Pendora decided to hold The Great Cannstatter Fest in August of 1908. The Cannstatter dated back to 1817 when, after two years of famine in Germany and most of the rest of the world caused by the massive eruption of Volcano Tambora in Indonesia in 1815, crops once again grew, and the harvest had finally returned.

The harvest celebration in Cannstatt, a city district of Stuttgart, has now become the second best reason to drink beer in Germany, after Oktoberfest in Munich. But it started out as a harvest festival, and that's what was being commemorated at Pendora Park in the summer of 1908, with Pendora's first Fruit Column.

Fruit Column Pendora Park, Reading Pa.

Located just east of the Shoot the Chutes, the Fruit Column of the Cannstatter Fest first appeared in August of 1908, and again in August of 1909.

The Cannstatter Volksfest in Stuttgart in 2004. A bit more elaborate than the Fruit Column on the previous page, but very similar, and almost 100 years later. (Photo from Wikipedia)

Today's Cannstatter Volksfest in Germany is celebrated over three weekends from late September to early October. The Cannstatter Fest at Pendora in 1908 ran for one week.

The Pendora Fruit Column of 1908 was created by Louis Hermann of Reading, who had created similar edible towers in Philadephia, at a cost of around $1500. The Pendora version cost only $800, yet most who were familiar with Mr. Hermann's previous works considered this to be his masterpiece. It was a lot more complex than it appears at first glance.

The fruity tower rose to a height of over 40 feet, and was topped with a design made of palm leaves, to which a variety of small fruits were fastened. The crown also held a sheaf of wheat, a nod to the harvest festivals of old.

The decorations were made entirely of fruits and vegetables and grains. What many considered to be the finest part of the work was the coat of arms of Pennsylvania on the south side of the base. In the coat of arms, the white horse was made entirely of peanuts, and the black horse of prunes and raisins, recreating the coat of arms in incredible detail.

On the north side of the column, the coat of arms of the United States was outlined with larger fruits and vegetables. The red stripes of the shield were made of red peppers, and the white stripes were made of onions.

Several hundred varieties of fruits and vegetables were employed, including more than 100 varieties of apples. No one counted them, but estimates put the total number of pieces on the column at 10,000.

Although the speaker at the opening, William F. Remppis of Reading, alluded to the harvest roots of the festival, he did not mention the volcano or its resulting famine, but instead described the festival as a way to "stimulate and encourage agriculture". The crowd on the opening day of the festival was estimated at 7,000.

The festival, and the fruit column, drew thousands of visitors to Pendora for that week in August. In addition to the sight of the column, visitors were also treated to music by the famous Liederkranz chorus, directed by Professor George Haage, and a concert by the Germania Orchestra. The sounds of the singers, augmented by the orchestra in the bandshell, were broadcast naturally by the band shell, without the need for artificial amplification, to all parts of the park.

For the sake of those familiar with the Liederkranz chorus and German music, and there are many in these parts who are, the selections included: "Die

Wacht am Rhein", "Schaefer's Sonntagslied", "Margarethe", "Landerkennung" and others.

The festivities through the week also included athletic events, including gymnastic exhibitions, putting the 12-pound shot, the 440-yard run, acrobatic events by Turners, and much more. Many events offered prizes. Admission was five cents for adults, and free as always for children.

There had been a Cannstatter Volksfest in Lauer's Park in Reading ten years earlier, but it only ran two days. It did, however, feature a fruit column. (See the ad near the end of the book).

William Remppis, narrator for the first Cannstatter Fest at Pendora Park.

Very little more is heard from Pendora for the remainder of the 1908 season. Advertising was placed at a minimum after the Cannstatter Festival, and limited mainly to one or two-line ads promoting the skating rink.

It would appear that the cost of the new attractions for 1908 had been crippling for Arrowsmith, and although 10,000 people had turned out for opening night, the crowds dropped off dramatically after that. It's almost as if visitors, upon seeing what was new at Pendora for the new season, then turned their attention to Carsonia Park once more.

Carsonia spent much more improving their park for 1908 than Pendora had, but they could absorb the cost. Apparently, Pendora could not.

In December of 1908, an article appeared in the Reading Eagle announcing that a planned sale of Pendora Park had been postponed. There was a judgement against Pendora filed by one its creditors, in the amount of $8.911.50, owed to the George F. Lance Company. A number of prospective buyers were disappointed that the sale was being delayed. January 5, 1909 was set as the date for the return of the sale.

Who was the creditor owed so much money by the Arrowsmith Amusement Company? The name rang a bell with me, and upon checking in Morton Montgomery's 1909 "Historical and Biographical Annals of Berks County Pennsylvania", I found the answer. Except for a few years spent as manager of the struggling Neversink Mountain Hotel in the late 1890's, George F. Lance had been in the lumber business.

George Fritts Lance, as manager of the Neversink Mountain Hotel in 1896. (Courtesy of Douglas Lance Fritz, great grandson)

With all of the additional construction at Pendora Park in 1908, especially the expansion of the roller skating rink (and its many yard feet of premium hardwood flooring), Arrowsmith must have run up a considerable debt to the lumber yard.

As far as Arthur V. Arrowsmith was concerned, the end of Pendora Park, or at least his ownership of it, was near. However, his Secretary, William Sweney, who was a machinist with a lot of recent experience with amusement parks, had his own ambitions for the park.

Before we turn over the calendar page to 1909, let's take a closer look at Arthur V. Arrowsmith, and how the Pendora Park chapter was very typical in his life story.

Old token found at Pendora (Larry Soltys)

Arrowsmith

Arthur V. Arrowsmith was a very interesting and complicated man.

Born in Easton, Pa. in 1860, Arrowsmith became very adept at a new skill, electricity. He was the superintendent of the Reading Electrical Construction Company, eventually becoming General Manager of the firm, last located at 904 Penn Street. In 1892, he wired The Junior Fire house for 30 incandescent electric lights, wiring them so that they would go out whenever the station's fire alarm went off. There doesn't seem to be a lot of logic in that- maybe a fireman could explain it to me.

Arrowsmith was constantly in the Reading papers, with records of his property transactions appearing every few months, or sometimes more often. He seemed to be adept at a skill which is now referred to as "flipping"- buying properties at bargain prices, doing his electrical magic on them (wiring for electric lights mainly), and then selling. This was going on before, during and after his tenure as head of Arrowsmith Amusement Company.

An early example of domestic wheeling and dealing was in 1907, when he sold his two-story brick house at 1380 Perkiomen Avenue for $4,500, while at the same time buying three two-story brick houses, at 613, 615 and 617 Eisenbrown Street for the same total amount- $4.500. It was basically a swap- three houses for one. A man named Herbert V. Landis was on the other end of those transactions.

In 1905, Arrowsmith was sued by Jacob B. Fricker in connection with a farm he had agreed to sell to Arrowsmith in 1903. The purchase price of the farm, including 216 acres in Robeson Township, was $16,500. The farm included the stock, consisting of 66 cows, heifers, mules, horses and farming implements. Apparently, the arrangement did not include the imparting of any knowledge of farming by Fricker to Arrowsmith.

Payment by Arrowsmith was to be made in $5.400 cash, $6.000 in preferred stock of the National Brass and Iron Works, and a mortgage of $5.000. After a small deposit of 100 dollars, Arrowsmith failed to pay anything, and did not take out the mortgage. It appears that Mr. Arrowsmith actually worked the farm for a year or more.

In his defense, Arrowsmith claimed that Mr. Fricker had defrauded him, claiming that income on the farm would be $3,000 a year. But Arrowsmith claimed that he actually lost money on the farm. The judge ruled against Mr. Arrowsmith, who had to pay 900 dollars, and ownership of the farm reverted to Mr. Fricker, who actually knew how to run a farm. Mr. Arrowsmith apparently thought that if he could string electric lights, he could do anything. He couldn't, but he was very good at electric lights.

In 1902, Charles S. Banghart, electrical engineer for the United Traction Company, designed a novel electrical effect for the roof of the Carsonia Park Theatre. The effect, using electrical lights, would give the roof the appearance of continually rolling, like the waves of the sea.

The plan, originated by Mr. Banghart, was constructed by a future Carsonia competitor. The Arrowsmith Electrical Construction Company, under the personal direction of Arthur V. Arrowsmith. Up until that time, Mr. Arrowsmith had mainly been an electrician, and it's possible that the Carsonia Park project may have instilled in him an interest in amusement parks.

One of his less than remarkable property transactions was the sale of a two-story brick home at 415 Orange Street for 75 dollars in 1912.

He married Sarah D. High, of 1045 Franklin Street on New Year's Eve, 1896. His residence at that time was 34 South 11th Street, only a block and a half away from his new wife.

On a day trip to Cape May, New Jersey in 1903 with the Reading Press Club, Arrowsmith, who was an excellent swimmer, broke away from the bulk of the visitors from Reading and enjoyed the Cape May beach. While there, a man got into the water a bit too deep, and began screaming for help. The lifeguard went to help, but was not able to rescue the man. Mr. Arrowsmith sprang into action, and, though he struggled a bit, was able to save the man. He had quite a story to tell the Press Club on the return train to Reading.

Arthur also tried his hand at politics briefly, running for Common Council in the Third Ward. He came in last among three candidates, attracting only 19 votes in all, compared to the first place winner's total of 300.

Although Pendora Park was Arrowsmith's biggest financial venture, it certainly was not his only one, and none of them seemed to be a big success. On August 26, 1907, near the end of his first year as the President of Arrowsmith Amusement Company, Arthur sold the "good will, stock and fixtures of his electrical business on Penn Street to former employees.

Despite selling off the Reading Electrical Construction Company in 1907, Arrowsmith continued to operate as an electrician under other company names, such as Arrowsmith & Co. Inc., A.V. Arrowsmith, S. S. Arrowsmith, and P. K. High (his wife's maiden name). In 1910, those companies were the subject of a lawsuit by L. P. Clark and Co., which was owed money for merchandise. In testifying, Mr. Clark said, "I have known Mr. Arrowsmith for about 15 years, and visited him once a month. He told me that the company had plenty of assets, more than enough to pay all of its obligations. Later, he met me on the street and said things did not look so favorable."

During the course of the inquiry, it was revealed that, although the electrical company was capitalized at $10,000, only $1,000 had actually been paid in by the partners. Asked where the other $9,000 might be, Arrowsmith replied that the "book accounts" were worth $3,000, and $5,000 was "good will".

The inquiry also revealed a slew of sloppy accounting practices, and a long list of debts, some of which had been "overlooked".

One can only wonder how much of the $100,000 capitalization of Pendora Park had been "good will".

Arrowsmith was an interesting character, and must be admired for his ambition and his marketing skills.

1909

Not Sold, Then Sold

For amusement parks in general, 1909 began on a sad note, with the death of Gustave A. Dentzel on January 24th. He was the inventor of the modern carousel, and its largest manufacturer in the U.S. Some of Dentzel's carousels, including the second at Pendora, cost as much as $20,000. He also built the second carousel at Carsonia Park. His Carsonia carousel appeared in 1904.

For the Arrowsmith Amusement Company, 1909 was beginning pretty much the same as 1908 had ended. From July, 1908, Arrowsmith had been failing to make payments on the mortgage for the Pendora Park property, and suit was being filed for recovery of the debt owed by Arrowsmith in the amount of $8,101.36. Due to the intervention of the previously mentioned Mr. Lance, the proceedings were postponed, first until January 6th of 1909, and then again for a few months. Meanwhile, the mortgage holder, Pamelia C. Sweney, William's mother, was instituting foreclosure proceedings for $22,500. The foreclosure was joined by another property owner, Mr. Frank S. Livingood, in the amount of $2,500.

Finally, in early April, the long awaited sheriff's sale took place at the Reading Exchange. Both parcels of property were sold at auction.

The first parcel, referred to as the "Pendora Park property", included 6 1/3 acres, and a two-story frame dwelling (more on that later). It was sold by Sheriff John C. Bradley to Garrett B. Stevens, representing Pamelia C. Sweney, for $11,000 dollars. Improvements on the lot included "a merry go round, an open pavilion (probably the one that housed the original carousel), an amusement building, a bandshell, chutes, miniature railway bed, columns, stands, etc."

The property in question also included two swans, four monkeys, two bears and six birds, which were apparently added to the park's attractions in 1908. These were being cared for by Frank S. Selak of South Fifth Street. The proceedings featured accusations from all parties involved.

The second parcel, which had originally been owned by Mr. Livingood, included two acres and 84 perches, and was located in the upper corner of the park area near Mineral Spring Road and 18th Street. This parcel included "three animal cages, one frame chutes and an amusement building." This was sold to T. K. Leidy, representing William P. Sweney. The price was $2,825, and there was a mortgage on this parcel for $5,000. From these two sales, it appears that the total amount of land taken up by the amusement park interests was about 8 ½ acres, or about half of what the park would eventually cover.

All of these people were strangely woven together in a confusing quilt of interests. This became evident only one month later, when T. K. Leidy, who was listed as solicitor for William P. Sweney, A. V. Arrowsmith and J. ED. Miller, were about to make application to the Governor for the incorporation of "The Hippodrome Amusement Company", the object of which was "the construction and operation of amusement devices, consisting of carousels, chutes, skating rinks, scenic railways, etc." The intent was for the company to conduct Pendora Park.

So what did all of this mean? Was Pendora Park dead? Not at all! Opening day at Pendora was set for June 15 for the 1909 season, and the Reading Times reported that the owners had gone to "great expense in building and arranging" amusements for patrons.

The popular roller rink, under the management of James Schwartz, promised once again to be a big draw. A number of Sunday school picnics were said to already be booked for Pendora in 1909, and the opening promised to occur "in a blaze of glory".

This season would see the introduction of a new amusement section, called "The Pit", meant to replace the "Molly Coddle", and would be located behind the large amusement building, and "able to accommodate 5,000 people at one time." It was said that Pendora's "Pit" was only the second such attraction in the country, the first being the one at Revere Beach near Boston.

The Pendora Pit would include two spacious galleries, and was said to be "a sure cure for the blues". Those who had seen the Pit at Revere Beach attested that "it had any three ring circus beaten to a standstill." The inventor of The Pit promised Pendora management that this attraction could not appear "within 300 miles of Reading". That would appear to cover Carsonia Park. Admission to The Pit would be 10 cents.

One big advantage of "The Pit" was that it could be open rain or shine, since it was all under roof. Before the June 15th opening, the park "presented a busy appearance; carpenters, painters, mechanics and landscape gardeners doing their part in getting ready for the opening".

Other new attractions included "The Devil's Causeway", "The Leap Shutes" and "The Revolving Wheel of Fortune", which would all be free.

The opening did in fact take place on June 15, but without the promised "blaze of glory" or with a procession, which had set the stage for the two previous openings. However, the Cadet Band did board a trolley at Second and Penn and rode to the park, playing along the way.

The evening's glee was somewhat marred by an accident, when 15 year old Peter Elwood Diehm of South 18 ½ Street broke his leg while going down the shutes (sic). Other attractions that were doing a brisk business opening night included the merry-go-round, the shooting gallery, moving pictures, the penny arcade and the miniature railway.

Despite the ownership of the park transferring back to the Sweneys in the mortgage foreclosure, Mr Arrowsmith was evidently still held in high regard by Mr. Sweney, because Arrowsmith appeared at the entrance to the park on opening night, 1909, greeting patrons with a smile, although opening day turnout was only about 1,800, a far cry from the 20,000 a few years before.

Things appeared to be going well a few weeks into the season, as Cassady's minstrels opened in "the pretty little theatre in the corner of the park", perhaps the "amusement building" that had been referred to in the sale of the smaller Pendora parcel.

A "large audience" was on hand at the theatre to enjoy the "blackface men who made a hit from start to finish." As the season wore on, management promised to present "an elephant on skates on Thursdays and Fridays.

Also, due to popular demand, a picnic ground had been created on "the terrace on the Mineral Spring Road side of the park", which would be the later site of the Reading Zoo.

In August, another Fruit Column was constructed for another Cannstatter Fest, billed this time with just a touch of hyperbole as "The Greatest Event in Reading's History!" Admission remained 5 cents in the afternoon, but was raised to 10 cents in the evening.

In September of 1909, Pendora offered a "handsome prize" in their annual Baby Show. And the popular aerialists continued to perform. Still, after Labor Day, the Reading Eagle mentioned heavy traffic to Carsonia and the mountain railways. No mention of Pendora.

News coverage in the Reading Times continued, but as far as the Reading Eagle was concerned, Pendora Park no longer existed. This goes well beyond the point where it could be explained by an oversight. Perhaps Pendora owed money to the Eagle also.

After a less than stellar season, the Allentown Democrat reported that "Pendora Park, Reading may be turned into winter quarters for 30 wild animals of a traveling circus." Something similar was indeed in the near future for Pendora Park, but nothing to do with a circus.

Another token coin found at the site of the Pendora Park amusement area. Courtesy of Larry Soltys.

Cannstatter Fest ...AND Fruit Column

All Week, Aug. 16 to 21, at

PENDORA

Greatest Event in Reading's History

PROGRAMME

Opening Ceremony

Monday at sunset, tolling anthem on the chimes of the Pagoda, Mt. Penn, by a native Chinaman, followed by a selection by four cornetists from the balcony of the same place.

Monday Night

Paine's Fireworks and Band Concert.

Tuesday Night

Unveiling of the $1,000 Fruit Column. Chorus by 50 members of the Liederkranz. Band Concert—50 men.

Wednesday

Paine's Daylight Fireworks in the afternoon at 5 o'clock. Paine's Fireworks in the evening. Gymnastics and Field Athletics. Band Concert.

Thursday Night

Chorus of 80 Voices, led by Prof. Haage, Liederkranz, accompanied by Symphony Orchestra, Mrs. Anthony, Soloist.

Friday

Daylight Fireworks in the afternoon. Children's Carnival, evening. Watermelon Match, Pole Climbing, Egg Race, Eating Contests, Handicaps, etc. Fireworks.

Saturday

Grand Finale—Gorgeous Pyrotechnics—Paine's Grandest Display. Band Concert.

ADMISSION---Evgs. 10c, Afternoons 5c

A rare 1909 ad in the Eagle. Outside of this big splurge, Pendora kept its 1909 ads to tiny two or three-line reminders.

1910

Proof of the existence of Pendora Park in 1910 can mostly be found in legal notices in the Reading Times.

Although William Sweney had continued operation of Pendora as The Rose Valley Amusement Company, lawsuits were now being filed on behalf of Arrowsmith against the "Pendora Park Company", which seemed to be controlled by Pamelia C. Sweney.

One such suit, late in the summer of 1910, tried to determine the ownership of relatively minor property at Pendora. One group, worth of total of 589 dollars, included "the swan house, boats, rails and pipes in the "Molleycoddle", 54 theatre benches, 3,000 sockets, drop curtains and other personal property."

About the only money-making proposition left earning money at Pendora, in addition to "The Pit" which operated only in warm weather, was the skating rink, which still operated year round-thanks to a stove which heated the place in the winter.

1911- A Very Bad and Short Year

1911 began on an optimistic note for Pendora owner William Sweney. Even though he had scaled back the park drastically from the time he took the helm in 1909, focusing only on the amusements that made good money with low overhead, there were plans for a revitalization. A man named Dodson, an amusement park owner from Columbus, Ohio, was due to arrive in February, with plans to lease Pendora Park, and restore it to its previous status as a first class amusement resort. That's something that Sweney never had the money to accomplish, and probably not the expertise either. Although Mr. Sweney had begun his association with Arrowsmith lending mostly enthusiasm and mechanical skills, he had learned a lot over the past three years.

In the meantime, only the roller skating rink at the amusement section of Pendora was operating, and remained fairly popular. Although the days of the newspaper ad wars were long over, Sweney kept a regular, though tiny three-line ad in the Eagle advertising the roller skating rink which, unlike Carsonia's, operated year round. Admission to the rink was always free, but patrons were charged 20 cents to rent the skates for the evening. There was an organ in the building which provided music for the skaters. And there was also a stove to keep the skaters warm.

The rink at Pendora, which was leased at that time by Frank Fertig of Stony Creek, and managed by William H. Rohrbach of Reading, was open every Monday, Wednesday, Friday and Saturday evenings from 7:30 to 10:30 p.m., as well as on Saturday afternoons. On the evening of Monday, January 2, there was a good crowd at the roller rink. Around closing time, an argument and fight broke out between a couple of boys who were patrons that night. The boys "went at it fist and nail", and the crowd paused to watch the encounter. The fight caused the skating patrons to leave a little later than they would have otherwise.

At around 5:40 a.m. on Tuesday, January 3rd, Mrs. Thomas Hartman, who lived in a house on the northern part of the grounds, arose to fix breakfast for her family. She saw flames rising from the southern end of the amusement building, and sent her grown son William to sound the alarm. William ran around the lake, to the fire alarm box near the 19th Street entrance to the park. The fire was called in by William about 5:45, and in that time, he noticed that the Pit portion of the building had already been fully engulfed in flame, indicating that the fire probably began there. So the fact that there was a stove in the skating rink area was probably irrelevant to the fire, because the fire did not start in the skating rink.

A few minutes later, Chief George W. Miller, along with Reading firefighters, arrived at the scene, but too late to be able to save the structure from the inferno.

William P. Sweney, the owner, lived just a few blocks away at 172 Clymer Street, and heard the alarm. According to the Reading Eagle, Sweney "looked out the window, saw the reflection of the flames... and hurried down Mineral Spring Road", thinking that the fire was at Miller's Soap factory.

When he got about a block away from Pendora, that's when he realized that the fire was consuming Pendora Park.

Two police officers, named Kline and Roland, were on patrol in the area shortly before the fire was discovered. Officer Kline returned to City Hall around 5 a.m., and heard shortly after that Pendora was on fire. At first, Officer Kline thought it was a joke, but then he heard the fire alarm sound.

The fire department worked hard for more than five hours to get the blaze under control. Their efforts were slowed in part by the huge crowd which had gathered to watch. In fact, they did more than just watch. Some, especially youngsters, actually ran around in the fire for fun. Several were injured from fire hose water streams, and a few were even injured falling through charred wooden floors. Apparently, crowd control was not a particular strength of the Reading Fire Department at that time.

A Reading Eagle reporter, who was there at the scene interviewing several people, was approached by two boys- Theodore Ruther of Third and Walnut Streets, and Matthias Eisenbise, of 1333 Cotton Street. The boys said that they had been patrons at the skating rink the night before, and were among the last to leave.

While they were passing "The Pit" building, they saw two men, conversing in low tones- one had a mustache. "They acted very funny, hiding when they saw us coming." This was around 10:40 p.m. If these two men "acting very funny" were the the ones who started the fire, it's odd that the fire wasn't noticed until 5 o'clock the next morning. It wouldn't take six hours for a fire to become noticeable.

The fire completely destroyed the large organ which provided music for the skaters. Also ruined in the skating rink area were 450 pairs of skates, a soda fountain, and a cigar and confectionary stand.

The fire destroyed the refreshment room, where the original carouself had stood, the moving picture room, bowling alleys, the new carousel which was closer to the amusement building than the older one had been, and a shooting gallery.

The building with the heaviest losses was "The Pit", where the fire started. The building was worth $3,400, and had just been refitted and repaired, costing more than $1.500. The operators of the bowling alley carried a small amount of insurance, so the fire would not be a total loss for them.

The loss of the skating rink was also high. The rink had a double wooden floor, costing 90 dollars a thousand feet.

Reading, Pa. Amusement Building, Pendora Park.

To the rear of the Amusement Building (the one with the flag) was where the fire was started on the morning of January 3, 1911. Most, if not all of the strollers were added by the postcard artist after the photo was taken.

On the left is the original carousel, and behind it between the pillars, the Ocean Wave can barely be seen. It cost a nickel to ride the carousel.

The Amusement building also included a bowling alley, an ice cream stand, a cigar store, and "The Pit" area behind and below, which typically would include oddball attractions such as air blasts, electric shocks, rotating barrels, moving steps... attractions which would have made patrons look ridiculous, and placed in such a way as to be visible to patrons above, to draw interest.

The great Pendora Park fire commanded headlines in newspapers near and far, including the Harrisburg Telegraph, the Lebanon Courier and Semi-Weekly Report, the Allentown Leader, and even the Washington (DC) Times.

But it was the coverage in the local papers, the Reading Eagle, the Reading Times, and the Kutztown Patriot, which was so interesting in their varied accounts of the fire.

They all agreed on the narration of the events, but there were large differences in the details. For example, The Kutztown Patriot quoted Mr. Sweney as saying that, although whispers of arson had been heard, he firmly believed that the fire was accidental. Despite the fact that the fire started in The Pit, which had not been used since the previous summer, and despite the fact that the Pit had no heating source and the electric was not turned on, Sweney stated that the fire had been caused by an electric wire".

The Patriot described the fire as so intense, that "after only ten minutes, it looked as if all of East Reading was on fire. And they pointed out that there had been another fire at the same spot 12 years before, when the Sweney Ice house, connected to the dam, had caught fire just after it had just been filled for the season. Sweney also told the Patriot that the fire losses were about $25,000. So much for the Kutztown Patriot version.

The Reading Eagle and Times, on the other hand, had a different version. Mr. Sweney was quoted as saying, "I am emphatic in my belief that the fire is the work of an incendiary (arsonist). Everything burned up at once. The only things saved are the bandshell, the old carousel building (which was earlier reported as being destroyed), several pillars and the ballustrades."

He went on, "I took possession over a year ago, and I owned everything. I estimate my loss at between $10,000 and $15,000, but nearer the latter figure. I carried no insurance whatever on my property, except $500 on the cottage. (More on the cottage soon). Then he repeats that the fire "was most likely caused by an incendiary." Very odd.

The amusement park fire remains a mystery, and, although it's pretty obvious that it was a case of arson, no one was every arrested or accused of starting the fire. So whodunit?

Well, since people's motives don't usually appear in newspapers, and anyone who would have knowledge of the case is long gone, it's pretty much open to conjecture. And a little conjecture has never been something that I shy away from!

First, there were two boys who were having one heck of a fight in the skating rink the night before the fire. Could they have done it? Probably not, because the fire did not start in the skating rink. Also, two boys reported seeing men lurking behind The Pit building the night before. On the other hand, although the two boys who reported the sighting were identified, the two boys involved in the fight the night before were NOT identified. Could they have been the same pair?

Secondly, Mr. Sweney mentioned that a Mr. Dodson would be arriving in February with the intention of leasing the park. Could it be that the people who ran Carsonia Park knew of Sweney's intention of bringing in an investor? Although Carsonia Park didn't have much to fear from the less-competitive Pendora of 1909 and 1910, it would have more to worry about if a well-financed manager restored Pendora to its original dazzle in 1911.

The possibility of the fire being for insurance purposes makes no sense. Sweney had no insurance on the park, and so had nothing to gain by staging an "insurance fire".

Also, it doesn't make sense that a fire which was started at 11 p.m. did not really start blazing until six hours later. Perhaps those two mysterious men came back in the middle of the night, to carry out what they were discussing "in low tones" the night before.

Unless someone with information who reads this comes forward, we'll probably never know the truth.

Reading, Pa.   Carrousel showing Miniature Railway, Pendora Park.

This postcard view taken from the "cottage" shows the Amusement Building on the right, and the old carousel bulding left of center, with the miniature train about to cross in front. In the background is a house-less East Reading, which had not yet been developed east of 19th Street.

A ladder can be seen in front of the Amusement Building, used by aerialists to climb up onto the high wire which was strung above the lake.

147

Reading, Pa.　Roller Skating Rink, Pendora Park.

Contrary to what this post card says, the roller skating rink is actually off the picture on the left. In the center background is another aerialist ladder, behind which is a good view of the Butt "cottage", which was the only part of the property that Mr. Sweney had any insurance on. It was not damaged in the fire. As usual, the Victorian looking strollers are purely postcard-maker fiction.

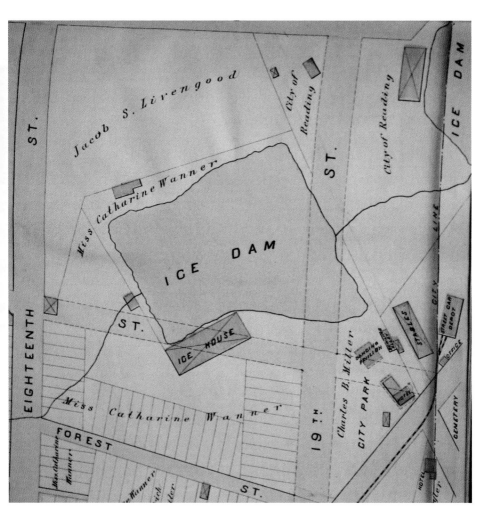

This is the Pendora Park area in 1884. The Ice Dam, which would soon be owned by the Sweneys, is in the same place as the park lagoon. The area on the right called "City Park" was also referred to as Miller's Family Park. News articles of the time often referred to Haak Street as the park's location. Just as it does now, Haak Street stops at Pendora, but it is shown here as a "paper street" going through the Ice House. (compliments of Sandy Stief)

The Sweneys, by the way, were often referred to in the press with the spelling "Sweeney", which was incorrect. There were Sweeneys in Reading, but these folks were not among them, and spelled their name without the double-e.

The Sweney family, including mother Pamelia, son William and his wife Annie, and his sister Ruth, all lived at 172 Clymer Street, in the custom of the day. Pamelia was a well known milliner (hat maker) who died in her 90's in 1923, and William was referred to in the City Directories as a "machinist", working at a business on Penn Street, even through his years as the proprietor and manager of Pendora Park.

It was common in the late 19th and early 20th Centuries for extended families to live together in the same house, especially if the house were a large one. And it was common not just for recent immigrants, but also for families that had been established in the area for some time. So it shouldn't be too surprising in the 21st Century to see extended families living together in the same house if it's big enough. If it's not big enough, the families themselves will discover that soon enough on their own.

This is the home occupied by the Butt family, before, during and after the heyday of Pendora Park. This is the house that can be seen in the center of the picture on page 162.

Mrs. Butt was the grandmother of Sandy Stief, to whom I am indebted for the use of this photograph. There are other pictures from the vicinity near the end of the book.

EAST READING DANCE FLOOR IN FLAMES

ORIGIN DUE TO DROPPING OF MATCH BY SPECTATOR

AT A BASKET BALL GAME ON WEDNESDAY EVENING, IS THE OPINION ADVANCED — ZOO ANIMALS NOT IN DANGER.

The big dance floor in the rear of the East Reading Hotel, formerly C. B. Miller's City Park Hotel, which, in years gone by, was the scene of hundreds of popular sociables, but is now used mostly for basket ball games, was discovered on fire at 9.25 a. m.

There was another fire in the Pendora Park area in 1911 that was almost as interesting as the big amusement park fire in January. This one, as headlined on this article in the Reading Eagle on October 12, happened at the East Reading Hotel, formerly Charles B. Miller's City Park Hotel, later called the Pendora Hotel.

The hotel had a very large dance floor inside, which was used for lots of social events, but was also a popular spot for basketball playing.

When the fire alarm was sounded after 9 a.m., it attracted the attention and a visit from L. H. Clewell, the head painter at the nearby East Reading Car Barn (where East Reading trolleys had been stored, and were now painted). The landlord of the hotel, William F. Horn, also made a hasty return to the hotel from back behind the nearby Gravity Station, where he was picking chestnuts.

The fire, which was probably started by a lighted match dropped by someone attending a basketball game the night before, was put out before it could do much damage, thanks in part to it's being discovered early, and in the daytime.

Shortly after the alarm, there was a report that the buildings of Pendora Park that had survived the big fire the past January were ablaze, and that there was danger to the zoo, only about 200 feet away.

The report turned out to be a rumor, but it made me wonder whether it referred to the small zoo that had been established in the amusement park years before. But this was a different zoo.

The Reading Zoo in Mineral Spring or Pendora Park

Ever since around the time of the short-lived zoo in the Pendora Park Amusement buildings, about 1908, there had been interest in establishing a City zoo. And the man who deserves the most credit for making that happen was Colonel Henry W. Shoemaker.

Col. Shoemaker was a banker, diplomat and a newspaper publisher. His newspaper ventures included one in Reading. In 1908, he purchased the Reading Times and Dispatch, and changed the name to the Reading Times.

He was fascinated by the wildlife in the Berks County area, and wrote many articles about animals, which were published in his Altoona Times-Tribune.

Around 1910, there were bounties for large predators, like the mountain lion, bobcat, wolf and coyote. Shoemaker was strongly opposed to these bounties, which he considered to be "a waste of the state's money". He argued that the predators removed aging and sickly prey, and kept the deer herds in check- something we're still trying to do today. Shoemaker had some sympathetic ears on City Council for a zoo, so he got right to work.

LIEUT. COL. H. W. SHOEMAKER,

In July, 1911, the site for the new zoo was chosen-about an acre of ground in what was then Mineral Spring Park. Even in the days before the Pendora Fire, the City owned the land northeast (uphill) from what is now deep left and center fields on the baseball field. So everything from the rise back was considered to be Mineral Spring Park.

The zoo was located in the slightly elevated area behind where the fielder in the yellow shirt is standing. The infielder is standing about where the Shoot The Chutes came down, and the outfielders are standing in the bandshell area. Before the viaduct was built, Mineral Spring Road came down from the left in front of where the viaduct sits, and over to Mineral Spring Park, where the road got its name. The old road is still there, but is blocked by a gate.

Work began on the zoo runs in July of 1911, but the Colonel couldn't wait. He shipped an elk to Reading, and it arrived about two months before the zoo would be able to accommodate it. So the elk was kept over in City Park for the time being, presumably to keep the bronze elk at the water fountain company.

The Colonel was updated on the timetable for the zoo's completion, near the end of August, and plans were made to ship the rest of the animals which would make up the initial nucleus of the zoo- two deer and a fawn, another elk, a black bear, two prairie wolves, a raccoon, an opossum, a great horned owl, and an English raven. One of the deer was an albino.

In the meantime, the runs were being constructed by park commission employees. They were to be about 100 feet square to provide plenty of room for the animals to exercise. On August 24th, the elk, by now named "Billy", was moved from City Park to his new home, and seemed to enjoy his 30x90 foot section of the enclosure much better than the cramped quarters over at City Park. Colonel Shoemaker was informed that more animals could now be sent, and citizens were encouraged to contribute animals from time to time. Reading's "little zoo" was on its way.

In fact, just about every newspaper account in the early days of the zoo referred to it as "Reading's Little Zoo". It's hard to say whether it was from embarrassment that the zoo was so small, or maybe it was pride, as in "it's small, but it's a fine zoo". Kind of like Reading's Charlie Brown Christmas tree in 2014.

Children really loved it, and would gather there after school hours in the fall of 1911. A cage on a slab of concrete was for the small black bear, which the children called "Teddy", and the bear seemed to respond to his name when called. The animals were most active between 4 and 5 p.m., anticipating feeding time. Once they were fed, they would lie down and ignore visitors.

An October 1911 article said that the pens were arranged so that additional ones could easily be accommodated. It was anticipated that within a year, many more animals would be added, including snakes.

To justify the zoo's cost of something less than $1,000 by the end of 1911, it was noted that New York City spends $182,000 a year on its zoo, not including donations, and that zoos in London, Paris and Berlin cost even more.

In the Zoo,
Mineral Springs Park, Reading, Pa.

When this postcard was printed, the zoo was in
Mineral Spring Park. But once the city bought
Pendora for a playground in 1918, it was located
within Pendora, which was expanded uphill to
almost where the viaduct now sits. Just to the right
of the cages is Rose Creek before it had stone wall
sides.

Everything seemed just ducky at the zoo, at least
until the first winter set in. In January, 1912, the
black bear died of an unknown cause. It was noted
that the bitterly cold weather had affected the

animals, "despite the fact that they have good quarters."

In April, another addition was announced. William H. Luden, Reading's confectionary giant, donated three pairs of European white swans to the zoo, along with two pairs of American whistling swans. Shipment was expected by mid-May, so there wasn't much time to build pens for the birds, which would be placed just uphill from the cages, on the lower dam on Rose Creek. There were two dams on the creek, one just below the Mineral Spring Hotel, and the second just above the zoo, where the tennis courts and now the skateboard park is located.

Eager as the zoo was to expand, not all donations of animals were welcomed. In July, 1912, Dr. Walter A. Rigg, one of the United Traction Company Rigg brothers, hailed police sergeant Kissinger and handed him a box, which contained an alligator. The 15-inch reptile had been sent to Dr. Rigg anonymously from Florida. When the policeman took the animal to the mayor, it was decided that the City was not in a position to care for the animal, and it was returned.

This view of the lower Mineral Spring Dam shows the Gravity Station across 19th Street in the background. The duck pond was here when the zoo was built, and the swans that were donated by Mr. Luden were placed here. Pens for the swans were built along the shore of the pond. Much later, this dam was removed, and Rose Creek was allowed to flow naturally down into Pendora Park. (from The Passing Scene)

So who sent the alligator to Dr. Rigg from Florida? According to the shipping company, a good possibility was Arthur V. Arrowsmith, who was living in Florida at the time.

John Jacob Roth

In a 1998 article in the Historical Review of Berks County, J.R. "Bob" Smythe, who was 80 at the time and relative of Sandy Stief, recalled what life was like at "Grandpop's" house. Grandpop was John Jacob Roth, who was the caretaker of the Pendora Zoo.

Mr. Roth lived in a stone home just up the hill and to the west of where the zoo was located. The house was on land that was owned by the City of Reading.

Mr. Smythe described the two bears, Ted and Rose. Sometimes, the cage door would be left ajar, and the bears would wander, especially Ted. There was a path that led from Mr. Roth's house over to their uncles and cousins, who lived in the cottage at the back end of Pendora Park's amusement section.

Mr. Roth would put a rope around Ted's neck and walk him home. One day, Ted wandered all the way down through Aulenbach Cemetery, and over to the lawn of Lutz Funeral Home! Once again, Mr. Roth to the rescue.

A gardener for the city, Mr. Roth was also the zoo caretaker. He also had a garden in front of the house, and neighbors were welcome to come up and share the fruits of the garden. There was also a spring under a grape arbor, and city policemen would stop to water their horses at the spring.

Mr. Roth was also a member of the Rainbow Fire Company. In 1926, he was fighting a fire at the American House at 4th and Penn. Roth was on the third floor balcony when it gave way, and he fell to the sidewalk. He was taken to the Homeopathic Hospital on North Sixth Street, and two days later, he died.

Mr. Smythe, Mr. Roth's grandson,who was also a volunteer fire fighter, later responded to a fire at Reading Steam Heat on Elm Street in 1958, when he fell off an ice-coated roof and landed in the alley between a church and the burning building. He was laid up for six months, and was put back together by Dr. Cedric Jimmerson. This part really hit home for me because, when I was twelve, my appendix burst, and I was rushed to the hospital surgery at Community General Hospital with only a 50-50 chance of survival. I was saved by the same but older Dr. Cedric Jimmerson.

Yes, it really is a small world. But before I return to the zoo, just one more story about Mr. Roth. He was a bit eccentric, and loved to ride his motorcycle with a sidecar. In 1917, he lost control on a ride, tumbled down a 15-foot embankment into a creek below. The accident would have mangled many men, but Roth came out uninjured!

The home of John Jacob Roth, complete with garden and grape arbor. Removed to make way for the Lindberg viaduct in 1927. (photo courtesy of Sandy Stief)

John Jacob Roth and wife getting ready for a ride @1915. This would have been taken right out front, under the grape arbor. The spectators on the porch are unidentified.

Note: in 1920, Roth was badly bitten by two coyotes who escaped from their cage. After attacking Roth, the animals were on their way toward the residential part of the city when officers rounded them up and shot them. (photo courtesy of Sandy Stief, great-granddaughter of Mr. Roth)

And now, back to the zoo.

Meanwhile, the zoo continued to grow. The two wolves that Col. Shoemaker had given to the zoo were now eight. So when the Colonel brought two pairs of rare black squirrels, he was given several wolves to take along. The zoo simply had too many of certain animals.

In 1913, four wild geese were on their way to the zoo, and would be placed on the lake with the swan.

Some of the incoming animals were actually replacing ones which had been lost. Despite earlier claims that the animals' quarters were sufficient for winter, a deer and a bear froze to death in 1912, and to replace them, Shoemaker was sending an English fallow buck, two young black bears, a horned owl, and a female opossum.

Later, Shoemaker sent a pair of his greatest loves, two wildcats from the Adirondack Mountains.

In 1913, the buck elk, whose mate had been on display at Carsonia Park and was donated to the Reading Zoo by the Traction Company, was in an especially bad mood because of the season, attacked and killed his mate, to the horror of neighbors and visitors.

Oddly enough, just a few years later, a reporter covering an elks convention (of the human variety) told of the purple and white elks' visit to the Reading zoo, and related tales of elk bliss in the pen since the buck elk, "Bill", had arrived at the zoo's opening. It told of a "little Bill" being born, and then Col. Shoemaker delivering two elk fawns to make the family a fivesome. Apparently, the original female was replaced in the interim, and all was forgotten.

Not all of the animals were large and ferocious. In July of 1912, twelve big frogs which had been caught at Dauberville were offered to the zoo, including one with five legs. The unfortunate frog's fifth leg was fully grown, and located in the middle of his back.

A 1918 Times article related that Shoemaker had just presented the zoo with three beautiful pheasants. Parks Superintendent Hoch was no doubt trying his best to appear appreciative, but at the same time was up to his eyeballs in excess animals. Feed prices were high, some materials were in short supply because of the war, and space in the zoo was limited. There was even talk of moving the zoo uphill into Mineral Spring Park, but the cost would have been prohibitive.

So the City put a number of excess animals up for sale, including spare coyotes, deer and doves, at bargain prices. No takers. A Times article noted that the coyotes in the zoo were getting along "as well as the Bolsheviks in Russia".

Even trades were tried. In a swap that sounds like a recent Phillies deal, four coyotes were traded to a zoo in Ireton, Kentucky for unspecified animals to be named later. And a Wernersville man, Dr. John Wenrich, offered not one, but three alligators to the zoo. This time, there was a new mayor, Mayor Filbert, who actually considered accepting them. Municipal amnesia.

But the animals kept on coming. Shoemaker sent a pair of odorless skunks. How do you say "no" to the guy who founded the zoo? Still, there was no room or money for more.

Speaking of Bolsheviks, a 1919 Times article editorialized: "Whether it is a Russian bear, a Bolshevik bear, or the common black bear at the Reading Zoo, the bear family seems bent on destruction. A bear cub at the Reading zoo, born on February 9th, has just been slaughtered by its elders, and hardly a bone has been left." Continuing on a bit less politically, the reporter noted that three of the fallow deer had just been sold off to a party in Yardley, Pa. because of overcrowding.

The cramped conditions and animal deaths continued for a few more years. Some of the swans up on the dam had frozen to death, right where they were swimming in the water. Then, the talk turned toward abandoning the zoo altogether. The Humane Society was complaining about the neglect of the animals.

In an apparent vote against closing of the zoo, an article in June, 1924 noted that the closing of the zoo would not result in savings in wages for the city. The caretaker of the zoo, Mr. Roth, did his zookeeper duty in conjunction with his other duties; namely, gardening. The caretaker was also responsible for work at Mineral Spring and Pendora Park. For some, though, the impact of the loss of the zoo to the City was greater. The following editorial, which appeared in the Reading Times after the closing of the zoo, says a lot about who was really at fault.

Peculiar justice, you say? Couldn't happen in the United States? Couldn't happen in Reading?

Then consider this:

The city zoo under proper circumstances can be one of the greatest attractions Reading could offer its children.

But it is being doomed to die.

It is being doomed to die because it has been neglected.

It has been neglected by the city.

And, curiously, it is the city, the party responsible for the neglect, which now passes sentence on the zoo because of its own shortcomings.

Mr. City is judge as well as defendant.

"Because I have neglected to take proper care of the zoo," says Judge City, "some of the animals have died. It is my decision that because I am going to continue being negligent and neglectful, the zoo had better be discontinued."

And so it was. Mayor Sharman announced that the animals would be disposed of and the exhibit discontinued. A statement from the Humane Society read, "The animals are confined in quarters wholly inadequate and the situation is nothing more than the infliction of wanton cruelty... The first enclosure is occupied by two large deer which have no shade during the summer, as the trees in the enclosure are dead. During the winter, the enclosure is a mud hole, the deer wallowing in the mud to their knees... there are fourteen wire-enclosed cages, only five of which are occupied. The occupants of the others having died, presumably from starvation, neglect or exposure. In the first cage is a black bear which suffers terribly during the summer months from the heat. There is no shade whatsoever above this enclosure and, although there is a small swimming tank built into this enclosure, there is no water in it." It went on...

In May, 1924, the remaining animals in the Reading zoo were transported to the newly-forming Williamsport Zoo. Mr. Roth assisted in gathering and caging the animals for their impending journey. It was said that Rose, the female bear, entered her travel crate willingly, while Teddy fought for two hours before finally being captured and crated. The City of Reading announced that the abolition of the zoo would allow for expansion of Pendora Park. And although the paper boundaries of the park expanded, no use was ever made of the area formerly covered by the Reading Zoo. Today, the former zoo location is an occasional picnic location along the Rose Creek and is used very lightly.

The old Mineral Spring Road veered right at 18th Street and wound down this path. (photo- Druzba) Below, a better 1935 view. (courtesy Northeast Family Dentistry)

The Association

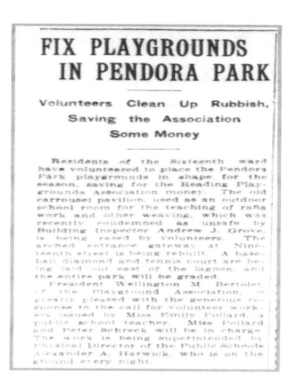

FIX PLAYGROUNDS IN PENDORA PARK

Volunteers Clean Up Rubbish.
Saving the Association
Some Money

Residents of the Sixteenth ward have volunteered to place the Pendora Park playgrounds in shape for the season, saving for the Reading Playgrounds Association money. The old carrousel pavilion, used as an outdoor school room for the teaching of rafia work and other weaving, which was recently condemned as unsafe by Building Inspector Andrew J. Grove, is being razed by volunteers. The arched entrance gateway at Nineteenth street is being rebuilt. A baseball diamond and tennis court are being laid out east of the lagoon, and the entire park will be graded.

President Wellington M. Bertolet, of the Playground Association, is greatly pleased with the generous response to the call for volunteer workers issued by Miss Emily Pollard, a public school teacher. Miss Pollard and Peter Schreck will be in charge. The work is being superintended by Physical Director of the Public Schools Alexander A. Harwick, who is on the ground every night.

1914 Reading Times story

It's time to give credit where it's due.

For the most part, the City of Reading has always had the best of intentions for the well-being of its citizens, in this case the kids of East Reading. But, as they say, the road to hell is paved with good intentions.

The City had grand plans for Pendora as a model park and playground, to be the rival of any park, anywhere. It initiated studies and designs that included sports facilities, a field house, a zoo, and swimming pools. Especially swimming pools.

But when push came to shove, the City has always seemed to lack the money to make that grand plan a reality, even in good times, and has often lacked the people with the passion and drive to make that grand plan happen. But, if Reading lacked the public servants with the passion to get things done at Pendora Park, that need for passion was filled as much as possible by the citizens of the Pendora Playground Association.

Immediately following the big fire of 1911, the kids of East Reading didn't need an official purchase agreement to start playing in Pendora Park. They swam in the lagoon when no one was looking. They swung on the swings left behind by Arrowsmith. And the City Playground department, sensing the inevitability of Pendora as a playground, took Pendora under its wing, although the Park did not belong to the city. They formed baseball teams, and volleyball teams, and competed with other playgrounds in the City, and they often won.

A Reading Times article from July 11, 1912, announced that the playground at Pendora Park, under the supervision of Miss Emily Pollard, was opened, and that "a large number of East Reading children were entertained during the day". It also noted that "swimming at Pendora Park will be too expensive a proposition for this season, and the movement to establish an up-to-date pool will be abandoned." Nevertheless, swimming instruction was being given on "Pendora Park Lake" from 2 to 5 pm on Tuesdays.

Actually, a proper swimming pool was ALWAYS part of the plan for the people in the area of Pendora Park, and for many in city government as well. There would be several studies done, with different pools at different locations in the park over the coming 30 years, each one appearing to be a sure thing, a foregone conclusion. In the meantime, though, the focus of the Association would be to get the park fixed up and safe for the kids, until the time when the City bought the property and took over maintenance of the park.

The Pendora Playground Association appears to have started around 1914, initially to help out the Reading Playground Association with money donations. Even back then, because of its layout, Pendora was actually TWO playgrounds- an upper and a lower one. The upper playground was centered around the stage and swings area in the vicinity of where Miller's Family Park had been. The lower playground was beneath the dam breast of the lagoon, where there were swings and pavilions.

At the time, the old carousel building, untouched by the fire, had been in use for some time as an outdoor school room for teaching weaving crafts. The building was condemned as unsafe by the Building Inspector, Andrew J. Grove, and was to be torn down- by volunteers, of course. (The City had no problem in condemning the building, but would not invest the money to actually remove it. After all, it was on private property!)

Those same volunteers were also re-building the arched entrance gateway at 19th Street, and plans were being made for a baseball diamond and tennis courts east of the lagoon.

Time and time again, residents of the area petitioned City Council to purchase the park for the City, fearing that if the City waited too long, the park would be cut up for building lots, as the newspaper article below points out. Considering what happened in 1950 to Carsonia Park, the fear was justified, as East Reading was growing and developing rapidly at the time.

WANT PLAYGROUND AT PENDORA PARK

Movement to Have City Purchase it Before it is Cut Into Lots

It is said that Council will soon be asked again to purchase Pendora Park and convert it into a public playground. It occupies a full block of space along Mineral Spring road, west of the Mineral Spring Zoo reservation, and was a popular amusement resort for several years. If the city does not buy or lease it for park or playground purposes, it may eventually be cut into building lots, as considerable building is going on in that vicinity.

In yet another Playground Association petition to Council in November of 1916, Association president Wellington Bertolet stated that "there is an average of from 350 to 450 children using the playground every day". It was said then that Council favored the purchase, and it was likely that some provision would be made in the 1917 budget. Same stuff, different year.

Up until this point, the desire of local residents for the city to buy Pendora as a playground was just a matter of common sense. But in July of 1916, another good reason presented itself.

In the wake of summer storms, Egelman's Reservoir overflowed late on July 21, 1916, and a torrent of water, mixed with stones and earth, five feet deep, rushed down Mineral Spring Park, within two inches of the door of the Mineral Spring Hotel, down to the lagoon in Pendora Park. The lagoon promptly overflowed, and the debris rushed over the dam breast, downhill to the Rose Creek outlet at 18th and Forrest, over that, and onward to Perkiomen Avenue.

The Reading Times related an "unprecedented and well nigh indescribable scene, when porches, remains of one-time pavements" and other things went drifting downhill to 16th, and on downhill to Muhlenberg Street.

The water continued downhill, along the same path as the underground route which carried Rose Creek Water to the Schuylkill, only this time above ground. In addition to tearing up the walkways and bridges in picturesque Mineral Spring Park, the flood also made a muddy mess out of Pendora, and City officials began to see the wisdom of buying Pendora Park, not only for playground use, but also to provide some flood control.

In March of 1917, it was announced by Mayor Filbert's office that the city will buy Pendora Park. The city had set aside $15,000 for the purchase, which would NOT include some land along Mineral Spring Road, which was to be used for building lots.

The city accepted this as natural, but the residents of the area worried that the development would swallow up their Pendora Park.

Despite what the City had said about the unlikelihood of a swimming pool at Pendora in 1912, the area residents had other ideas. In August of 1917, a huge festival was held at Pendora by the Pendora Improvement Association (the name would change from time to time).The festival, which attracted 2,500 people, raised more than 200 dollars. (that may not sound like much, but when hot dogs are selling for a nickel, it takes a lot to raise 200 dollars).

Fifteen Boy Scouts of the Mount Penn troop assisted in the patriotic ceremonies. "During the entire evening, the Pendora orchestra furnished music at the dancing pavilion", and the festival was to be continued for a second night. They even had their own orchestra!

Just to show how much the Association was in tune with the neighborhood, "the entire walk from the 18th Street entrance was illuminated by a continuous streamer of lanterns, so that people from Mineral Spring Road and Haak Street need not walk all the way around the block to the entrance at 19th and Cemetery Lane." Donations were starting to roll in for the swimming pool, which was the purpose of the festival. An account had been set up at The Pennsylvania Trust Company, so that swimming pool donations could be kept separate from the Association's other funds. The Supervisors of Parks and of Playgrounds were on hand to examine blueprints which had been drawn up for the swimming pool.

While the City was setting aside $15,000 in 1917 for the possible purchase of Pendora for a City Playground, the Pendora boys and girls, for the second time, won the annual playground track and field championships. Mrs. Sweney, owner of the land being used as a City Park, asked for property tax relief because of the City's use of her land as a public park. No decision. She really deserved it. If private land started being used as a playground by kids today, a big fence would be put up around it to make sure that no one got sued.

A new set of eight-swing baby swings and an eight-swing large swing outfit were added in 1917, along with lights to make the park more efficient at night... not courtesy of the city, but "the gift of Mrs. Isaac Hiester".

Again in 1917, there was talk of constructing a swimming pool, and while the city could only suggest help in this effort, actual money for the project was already being collected by the playground association. And the association was not the only group interested in a park, and a pool, for Pendora.

In September, members of the Olivet Club No. 3 put on some "snappy and catchy musical entertainment" in the basement of St. Andrew's Reformed Church, and the proceeds were turned over to the Pendora Park Association, which "will build a swimming pool at the playground next year".

Pendora was also being made a center for the war relief effort in 1917. Mothers in the neighborhood spent afternoons and evenings on Pendora grounds, working on sewing machines under the pavilion, making garments for our soldiers in France.

Throughout the history of Pendora Park, at least until the end of the 20th Century, the playground association always took the lead in raising money in the community, and raising hell in City Hall, to get things done in Pendora Park.

The City mostly answered requests with the standard "We don't have the funds available", and so the Association would raise the funds. That's how repairs got done, that's how lights were installed, and that's how benches were purchased.

The Association was not just a handful of people who gathered around someone's kitchen table. There were more than 20 active members, including the president, William F. Moser; Vice President, Edward Sproessar; Secretary A.H. Burgess, and Treasurer H. E. Williams.

As the City continued to delay purchase of the park, citing fears of cost overruns, the Association would not give up, on the park, or on the swimming pool. In a September, 1917 Association meeting, bills were paid "for the orchestra, lights, baseballs, trolley fares to and from baseball games, bats, shuttlecocks, repairs to balls, entertainment of visiting teams, etc." After the bills were paid, there was enough left to "invest $100 at three percent", with the entire sum going toward "the swimming pool fund."

Also at the meeting, it was announced that "Mr. and Mrs. Butt at the Pendora cottage", who were in charge of the playground gardens that were rented out to residents for 50 cents per year, would be taking reservations for 1918. The plots were being guarded after it was discovered that some boys were stealing tomatoes from their neighbors' plots.

Every week or two during 1918, there were newspaper stories about how the city was in the process of purchasing Pendora Park for playground use. There had been stories like this since 1914, but they never really amounted to anything, at least as far as the City was concerned. The Playground Association never wavered, holding one special event after another, either to purchase needed improvements to Pendora, or to have a swimming pool built, which they assumed would happen as soon as the city bought the park.

In a rather laughable attempt at a trade, the City offered a bill to appropriate $15,000 for the purchase of Pamelia Sweney's 6.267 acres of Pendora Park, "in exchange (for) a triangular lot of 1,062 square feet on the south side of Mineral Spring Road near Eighteenth and Nineteenth Streets, then owned by the city." If the 1,062 square feet figure is correct, and it's hard to believe that it is, then somehow Mrs. Sweney was to find a use for a little sliver of land that one would have trouble locating a double wide onto, and which would ten years later be condemned for the construction of the Lindberg Viaduct.

No surprise then that three years later, a Times story stated that Mrs. Sweney, 87, who was still living at 172 Clymer Street, was being treated to a *post card surprise* by her friends from First Presbyterian Church. Apparently, she was not impressed by the City's offer of this vest-pocket property up the hill from her park land. Mrs. Sweney apparently had some spunk. During World War I, in her mid 80's, she was one of the most faithful workers in her church's Red Cross unit.

The city's promises are what got the headlines. But when the long-awaited event finally occurred, it was buried in an article of other, unrelated city expenditures. Sort of like, "Oh, by the way, we now officially own Pendora Park". Did that mean the swimming pool was finally coming? Well, not the actual pool, no. The plans would continue, along with studies by landscape architects, cost estimates, and more contributions from civic groups. But no pool.

Meanwhile, in 1920, Mayor Stauffer "deplored the fact that the town had paid $15,000 for Pendora, and then did nothing to it." "Life", he said, "was too short to be deprived of the many good things that might be had by cooperation." (A good lesson for today's U.S. Congress).

In 1922, after years of fundraising and foot dragging and petitions, the issue of the pool construction finally came to a vote. And the answer, as usual, was, "we don't have the funding right now." It wasn't the first time the kids of East Reading would be deprived of a pool, and it certainly would not be the last.

Real Plans

One of the most promising and sensible of the city's pool proposals came in 1926, when they received the results of a plan for "The Development of Pendora Park into a Beautiful Playground", which was published in the Reading Eagle on September 11.

The report, prepared by Olmsted Brothers, landscape architects of Brookline, Massachusetts, was well thought out, extensive, yet not overly grandiose in scope. The plan, which would require adding some adjacent land, would increase the park's size to 16 acres in all.

On the sketch on the next page, notice the inclusion of the new viaduct, as yet unnamed, near the top of the sketch. The area left center is set aside for "coasting", as sledding was called at that time. More on that later.

The pool is located on the bottom left, with a wading pool bottom center. Just about everything else on the plan became reality.

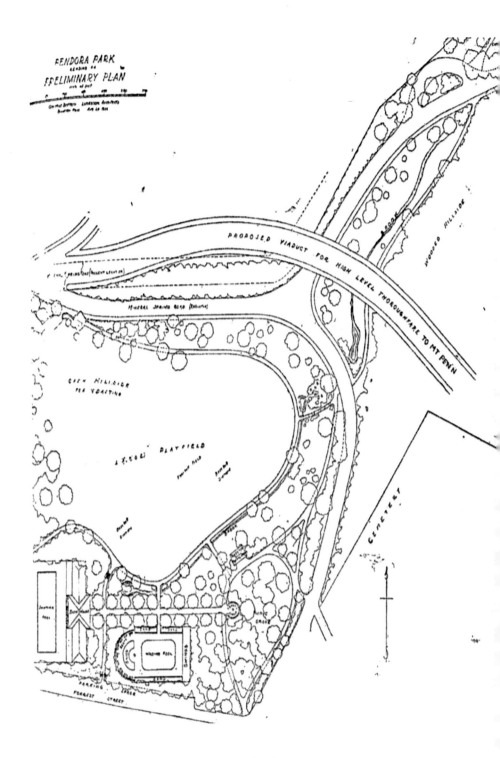

PENDORA PARK
PRELIMINARY PLAN

The city had for years accepted the necessity of better connecting Mineral Spring Road with Mount Penn. And plans were already in the works for re-locating Mineral Spring Road east of 18th Street to make room for the new Mineral Spring Road Viaduct, which would later be called the Lindberg Viaduct. This plan took that relocation into consideration.

The center of the park would be a large, informal green to accommodate baseball and football fields, much as it is today. Some of the trees in the northwest corner would be removed to provide for a coasting area (sledding in the winter).The land was already ideally sloped for this purpose, as Arrowsmith had seen many years before when he installed the Shoot The Chutes there.

The lower portion of the property, along Forrest Street, was where the really interesting stuff appeared. Over along 18th Street was a swimming pool, 50 by 150 feet, with an adjacent bath house for changing. This area would be fenced in, so that casual park visitors would not intrude on the privacy of the bathers. Additional parking for pool patrons would be provided by widening Forrest Street to make room for about 50 parking spaces.

Up along Forrest Street closer to the present Field house, about where the dinosaur park is, was to be the wading pool, a bullet-shaped area which included sand areas for play, and swings.

Rose Valley Creek would have been allowed to meander naturally through the park, above ground the entire way. It was a beautiful plan, and had plenty of supporters in East Reading, as well as a few on City Council. But not enough. Mayor Sharman, who had earlier favored improvements in the park, said that the Oldmsted plan would not even be considered until the following spring.

Much as Mayor Sharman was not wild about the Olmsted plan, he was rather fond of another plan by City engineer E. Clinton Weber, which combined several projects into one- namely, a swimming pool, and an "Aulenbach Relief Road", which was supposed to provide easier access between the City and Mount Penn. Apparently, this was being considered as an alternative to the Lindberg Viaduct project.

This plan, created by Amusement Development Associates Engineers of Philadelphia, called for a larger pool up at the former duck pond. (from the Berks History Center Library)

City officials apparently were very serious about this project, to the point that they even condemned land to accommodate it. In February of 1926, City Council approved plans to acquire the former Miller's Family Park property, complete with the Pendora Hotel, to become part of Pendora Park.

A Pool, and A Rutchie for Tillers?

This portion of the narrative will be an education in terminology for the younger reader, as it was for the writer.

In January of 1926, Reading Mayor Sharman announced his endorsement of a homegrown pool plan for Pendora, which called for a concrete pool, 75 feet by 300 feet, "taking in part of the Pendora swan pond." This area cried out for rehab anyway, and just about any plan for the swan pond, other than putting more swans in it, would have been seen as an improvement.

This plan, by the City engineer, also included the possibility of a large "rutchie" for children, almost 1,200 feet long. (Rutchie is a classic Pennsylvania Dutch term, and rhymes with "Butchie". A "rutchie", as it turns out, is a place where kids can go "coasting", or sledding in the winter. Of course, the Olmsted plan also called for a rutchie area, but it was made to seem like a fresh idea on this new plan.

A little searching about rutchies turned up some interesting facts, and terms. Rutchies are not necessarily purposely-made things, but can occur naturally, as a city street, for example. It was said that one of the best rutchies in Reading was Elm Street, but some folks disagreed.

Elizabeth Steely of Shanesville contributed her own view in March of 1926. "We used to rutchie from Hampden down to 8th, and didn't have to worry about the tillers being hit by machines or trolleys." OK, let me translate. First off, she's probably referring to Spring Street, which is one heck of a hill (or rutchie), and it's an awful long way all the way down to 8th from 13th, and very steep, too!

Secondly, we're introduced to another old term, "tillers", which are sleds or toboggans, or the people who operate them. What Elizabeth didn't mention were the "blockers", which were kids stationed at intersections to prevent disasters. Maybe that's why the tillers didn't get hit by machines (cars) or trolleys." My good friend Jack Holcomb, who's been around the block a few times, confirmed these definitions.

Determined as Mayor Sharman might have been for the project to be completed by the following year, his vision of a pool and rutchie at Pendora never came to pass. Still, there would be other pool proposals for Pendora.

1927 saw the construction of what eventually became known as the Lindberg Viaduct, although some were opposed to naming the structure after a man that some people felt was a "Nazi sympathizer". The original construction was quite an undertaking, and the re-construction in 2003 was almost as time-consuming, when Perkiomen Avenue once again became the main artery into Reading from Mount Penn.

Those two construction events, along with a number of suicides off the bridge in the 1930's, could be enough to fill a book- but not this one. Throughout the park's history, the viaduct has never really been considered part of Pendora Park, but rather just something that <u>overlooks</u> the park, so we won't include it here.

One has to stop somewhere. If I include the viaduct, then I include Mineral Spring Park, Egelman's, etc.

Children from all Reading playgrounds were welcome at Pendora for Play Day, 1936. Behind the children in the right background is the large stone wall behind the original softball field. The wall is much smaller now, and the softball field is gone. The girls in the foreground are standing on the present baseball field's infield. The hillside in background left is bare, because of extensive grading required for the viaduct. In the distant right background, the Rose Creek Waterfall. (Reading Recreation Commission)

Costume Parade

Depression era at Pendora Park. 1930. (Reading Recreation Commission)

Times are Tough, Again

The depression kicked off by the crash of 1929 meant hard times for just about everyone, and put many public works projects on hold, or in the dumpster. So it was inevitable that the third big swimming pool proposal for Pendora in the early 1930's would get shot down.

In the wake of the latest pool rejection was the fact that, in 1924, William H. Luden had donated $1,000 toward a swimming pool for Pendora which had grown to $1,250 by 1932. Once the pool had been rejected by the city, Luden suggested from his new home in Philadelphia that his donation might instead be used to purchase playground equipment for the city playgrounds

This same suggestion was made few months later by George M. Jones, a former Recreation Board member who was the holder of the Liberty bond containing the Luden donation. By the time this motion was acted upon a few months later, Recreation Department head Lantz saw the money as a way to fund some other unstated project. The matter was tabled, and it's unclear whatever actually happened to Luden's donation.

It should be pointed out though, that Pendora Park's swimming pools were not the only such plans on the drawing boards at the time. There were pools proposed at 11th and Pike, and a South of Penn Pool, and a real pipe dream of a pool near Gilson Alley.

Two of these pools got built, while Pendora and Gilson Alley did not. Though talk of the pools sounded good, especially in the summertime, many people never stopped to consider how much maintenance would be required.

Socialist Mayor Henry Stump and his supporters in early 1930's city government had a way of being big supporters for the City Pool projects while they were running for election, but suddenly becoming more conservative after the election. Even though there were members of the City Council who hated the idea of pools at the time, especially Councilmen Maurer and Hoverter, they were certainly open to other ideas of improvement for city parks. Especially if someone else was paying for them. Still, let us not forget that Mayor Stump was the only Mayor of Reading, Socialist or otherwise, who was ever elected to three terms. He was a very popular mayor. And he did a lot of good things for the people of this community, including Lake Ontelaunee. And, in addition to improving parks, he also created one, in Sinking Spring, originally called Socialist Park.

In all fairness, it should be pointed out, (and the city did point out) that in 1934, the citizens of Reading owed 1.4 million dollars in overdue taxes to the city. More people were out of work, so more people were unable to pay their taxes. And, without all of that tax money coming in, some things were just not going to get done. Because of the extreme economic conditions during the Depression, the Socialist Party (and the Communist Party for that matter) became popular across the U.S., and not just in Reading. It might be surprising for some to learn that, in the 1930's, Socialist and Communist parties also became a force to be reckoned with in Germany and Russia, among other countries. The Communists were ruthlessly exterminated by the Nazis in Germany, but they were firmly in power in Russia.

In the U.S., President Roosevelt began to initiate a number of public works bills designed to put people to work. A few of Roosevelt's programs were redundant, and some were just plain unworkable. But some were brilliant. And as some biographers have pointed out, nobody really knew exactly what to do to defeat the Depression. But everyone knew that something had to be done. And, to his credit, Roosevelt was willing to try things that looked promising.

Happy Days Are Here Again

One of President Roosevelt's New Deal recovery programs in the early 1930's was the PWA- Public Works Administration. It was similar in intent to the WPA, or Works Progress Administration, but the difference was in the way the work got done.

With the PWA, money was appropriated by the Feds to the state Emergency Relief Boards, and the state distributed the money to counties based on requests that were received for work projects. The projects were then put up for bid, and the contracts awarded based on low bids. WPA, on the other hand, hired the workers directly, and the work was paid for directly by the Feds.

In Pennsylvania, the State Emergency Relief Board distributed over 11 million dollars in PWA project funds to Berks County in 1934, which including much valuable work to the Pagoda skyline, which is still being enjoyed today.

In terms of Pendora Park, it meant grading work to create an athletic field, $15,000; masonry, spillway and channel completion, $15,000; curb and gutter work along 18th Street and Forrest Street, $3,500; and, not a swimming pool, but a wading pool- $4,000. Funds also allowed work to begin on development of a recreation center, or field house, not to mention $30,000 in much needed wages for local workers.

Of course, the desire of the citizens of Reading for swimming pools did not die easily. And once again in 1935, the City was urged by the Pendora Association as well as another East Reading community group to build a pool in their neighborhood. Another East Reading community group was pushing for a pool at the 13th and Cotton playground. I was surprised to hear about this, since I never knew there WAS a 13th and Cotton playground. But my dad and mom sure did!

I ran across a newspaper article from 1938 talking about a 4th of July festival that was held at 13th and Cotton playground. I didn't learn much about the playground, but I did discover that my dad was part of the entertainment that night, playing the accordion. (I've heard him. He was very good). A little farther down the article, I saw mention of my future mother, who was a safety patrol major, and also in charge of the sandbox. Neither one of them ever mentioned this to me, but I'm guessing that my dad at least had a crush on her at that point, since he lived over on Chapel Terrace behind the 12th and Chestnut playground, and she lived on 13th Street. So the mystery 13th and Cotton playground was in her neighborhood, not his.

I learned further that the 13th and Cotton Playground was on the site of a former elementary school, just as the 12th and Chestnut playground that my dad (and I later) played at had once also been an elementary school!

When I was growing up, I remember there being a gas station at the intersection of 13th and Cotton, and I guess that's where the playground had been before that. In any case, there was no pool built at 13th and Cotton. And, from the size of the lot that I remember, they would have been hard pressed to fit one of any size there anyway. No parking, either.

But, getting back to the Pendora Field House, I mentioned earlier that the PWA required work to be open to bids.

Raymond E. Kiebach later told the story about how the bids for the Pendora and Baer Park field houses needed to be advertised in the next day's paper or the funding might be lost, and the deadline had already passed. Mr. Kiebach used his "pull" to get the Reading Times to add a last minute advertisement in their morning paper, and the project ultimately went through.

In gratitude, Mr. Kiebach's name was included in the bronze plaque mounted in both the Pendora and the Baer park field houses as one of the people who deserved credit for the field house's construction. He didn't set a single stone, or hammer a single floor board, but without him, the field houses would never have been built.

Though the money had been appropriated for the Pendora wading pool, it would still take a few years until East Reading kids would be able to start splashing in it.

PARENTS BIG GIVERS FOR PENDORA PARK

Finance Benches, Part of Wading Pool Cost

One hundred benches. costing $300. were ordered for Pendora Park last night at a meeting of the Pendora Playground Parents' association. They will be delivered in time for the Fourth of July celebration, officers stated. The association also voted a payment of $250 towards the cost of a concrete wading pool. the city and the WPA to pay the balance.

Ralph Ruppert presided at the meeting. For July 4 the Pendora program calls for a baseball game in the morning, a Philharmonic band concert in the afternoon and soft ball play and fireworks in the evening.

June 1936 story in Reading Times told of the recently reformed Association's continuing efforts to raise money for Pendora, but this time focusing on a wading pool only, despite big bucks rolling in from Uncle Sam. Fireworks at Pendora were often the best in the City of Reading, no thanks to the City.

The Long Awaited Wading Pool

Despite a rainy Fourth of July, there was a lot to celebrate in 1937 in Pendora Park. The Pendora Parent Playground Association, re-formed just a few years earlier under the guidance of Ralph D. Ruppert, had become active again in pushing along some badly needed improvement projects in the park.

Although the Ringgold Band concert was cut short by the rain and the fireworks postponed, the park finally saw the dedication of its newest attraction- a 40-foot wide wading pool- its unpainted white concrete contrasting nicely with the green grass surrounding it.

Ex-Mayor Stauffer, himself from East Reading, was there to perform the dedication, joined by current Mayor Stump. Stauffer complimented the Pendora Association for its ongoing efforts, creating "one of the finest recreation areas anywhere."

The Association was busier than ever, working and raising money for tables, benches, a flag pole, slides, swings, see-saws, a merry-go-round and an ocean wave, the last two simpler versions of the ones that Arrowsmith had purchased 30 years before. In the planning stages were a permanent field house, already designed, along with a swimming pool and bath house (really? I thought that idea had already died at least twice!) But the wading pool could not be denied- it was here!

rma Roth, 9 (left), and Joyce Focht, 6 (right) are among the first to splash in the new Pendora Wading Pool in 1937 (Reading Times)

Pendora's Midget Leaguers, above, will endeavor to present the East Reading playground with its first Southern Division championship during the 1937 race of the Southern Division of The Times-City Recreation tournament. Kneeling, left to right, are: Assistant Coach Bob Brown, Charles Caruso, Ted Rechlin, Lawrence Delewski, Richard Glise, Earl Spencer, Ronald Brown. Standing: Donald Pasley, Jack Devlin, Don Hehr, Emmons Williams, Robert Abraham, Art Kline, William Calabria, Robert Bechtel, Coach Guy Rhein is missing from the picture.—Times Staff Photo.

1937 Pendora Midgets baseball team. In 1938, long- time Association leader Bob Duddy was the manager.

Giving Pendora's New Wading Pool a Christening

Hundreds of youngsters yesterday took the waters of the new Pendora playground wading pool for the first time to give it a good breaking-in. The pool, built with funds raised by the Pendora Parent-Playground Association, was dedicated with a ceremony yesterday. A sector of the spectators here is watching the first batch of waders go knee-deep into the virgin water.—Times Staff Photo.

By the way, in case you've ever wondered when that metal fencing backstop behind home plate was made, the answer is, once again, 1937. When I played there as a kid in the 1960's, it looked as if the backstop was still the 1937 original. I'm sure it's had some work done to it since then. Hasn't it?

My friend Larry Soltys' daughter Laura, 8, standing center under the sprayer in 1976. In the black trunks on her left is cousin Paul Szymborski. (Courtesy Larry Soltys)

A Bangless Fourth and a Field House

The 1937 Reading Times that featured those great pictures on the preceding couple of pages also had some pictures of kids burned by fireworks being treated in the hospital. That changed dramatically in 1939.

July 4th of '39 was billed as a "Bangless Fourth". Disregarding threats of court tests to the new state anti-fireworks law, Pennsylvania Governor James created what no one alive then could remember- a Fourth of July without unsupervised fireworks.

Anything other than paper caps were banned in the 1939 celebrating, with the exception of very tightly controlled and supervised fireworks displays, like the one the night of the 4th in Pendora Park.

It was the quietest Fourth since 1923, when Reading Mayor John Keim Stauffer had signed a tough anti-fireworks law for the City. That old law, which was largely ignored, was toughened by Mayor Stump. Gone also were those tents along the road where fireworks could be purchased. Gone were the lines of fireworks injuries in local hospitals.

In 1939, police were out on the roads in full force over the 4th, on the lookout for drunken or reckless drivers and speeders. Even old timers, who could remember the cannon being fired on Leinbach's Hill in West Reading, overlooking the Schuylkill, could not remember a 4th this quiet.

A postcard view from @ 1900 of the old Penn Street Bridge, taken from Leinbach's Hill in West Reading. Note the cannon in lower left, for 4th of July celebrations.

Reading-area attractions still drew their crowds, on both mountains, and at City parks, despite the fact that many people were out of town for a train or car trip up to the Big Apple for the New York World's Fair. Nobody seemed to mind the absence of unsupervised fireworks that much, since they had the Pendora fireworks to look forward to.

In the afternoon, Mayor Stump and Councilman Howard McDonough officially dedicated Pendora's permanent field house, a beautiful stone structure designed by noted local architect Alexander Forbes Smith, the kilted wonder, who had also designed the Baer Park field house, the McIlvain Pavilion on Neversink Mountain, and a nearly identical pavilion in Charles Evans Cemetery, among many other structures in the area.

The Pendora field house, as well as the Baer Park field house, were also both made from the stone from the old prison in City Park, which had been torn down in the early 1930's. No wonder it felt like a castle inside! The old jail had even LOOKED like a castle.

The previous summer, bids for the field house project had been accepted by the city, and the low bidder was Anthony R. O'Reilly, the former chief engineer of the Reading water bureau, at $19,495. This was almost $2,000 more than the low bid for Baer Park's field house, which was a little smaller.

If that amount seems like a bargain, consider the fact that, the same week that the field house was dedicated, a market in Reading advertised chuck roast for 13 cents a pound, eggs for 21 cents a dozen, pork and beans, 3 cans for 11 cents, and a pound of hot dogs for 17 cents. With prices like these as a backdrop, it's easier to appreciate that no one was cheaping out on the field house. It's a large building, and the price was something that the city alone would not have been able to afford.

The PWA covered 45% of the cost of the field house project- The City paid the rest. The same deal applied to all of the work done by the PWA. It was a win-win-win for the city. They got improvements they needed, only had to pay about half of the cost, and its citizens were put to work in the Great Depression.

This view of the field house under construction in 1938 was taken from Forrest Street, showing the rear of the structure. (Reading Recreation Commission)

The field house was not the only item on the list for Pendora that year- other improvement projects, including heating and ventilation, plumbing and drainage and electrical work, added another $7,000 on to the cost of improvement work.

Some of the improvement needs were not so expensive, and might have seemed to some to be not so critical. Thomas W. Lantz, the director of the city recreation department, was made aware of an acute shortage of playing cards at 11th and Pike and Pendora.

It might seem kind of foolish now, but it was the Depression, and the old or jobless men who gathered at the mostly completed field houses at the parks were in need of all kinds of playing cards, "except 'Old Maids'", thank you. Anyone who could donate "complete decks" of cards was urged to have them sent to Mr. Lantz at City Hall.

In June of 1939, the City was accepting bids for two cement tennis courts to be built on the site of the former duck pond (the site of the latest pie-in-the-sky swimming pool), and the accompanying stone bridge and stairway. Many things were happening at Pendora- just about everything except the long awaited pool. At least the tennis courts would not require much maintenance once they were built.

At one point in the early 1930's, the Pendora Playground Association, or something with a very similar name, had shriveled nearly out of existence, as it has a number of times in its history; but it was back to fighting strength in the late 30's, hopefully to stay.

The Association had grown to 250 members by 1939, and they became a force to be reckoned with in East Reading. Maybe its size was due to so many people still being out of work. If you're unemployed, you have more time for community matters. Although the association had failed to get a swimming pool built at Pendora, (again), they had succeeded in having a field house built, as well as a wading pool.

The Pendora Field House, as it appeared in 1939. (Reading Recreation Commission)

Two views of the field house in 2014. New windows, new doors, new roof, weeds growing out the east chimney. Oherwise, the same. (Druzba)

More than 250 members of the Pendora Parent Playground Association gathered in the center's new field house Friday night. Leaders and guests gathered around the table are, left to right, Mrs. Ambrose Bimson, financial secretary; Mrs. Claire Hoffman, Claire Hoffman, treasurer; Superintendent of City Recreation Thomas W. Lantz, Darlington Hoopes, Ambrose Bimson, vice-president, Mrs. Hazelett Hoopes, school board president; Ralph D. Ruppert, president of the association, and Mrs. Samuel Sailer. Ruppert was presented with a plaque during the meeting. — Times Staff Photo.

This 1939 Reading Times photo shows the leaders of the Pendora Park Association, gathered along with all 250 members, at the newly opened Field House. Standing far right is president Ralph D. Ruppert. Seated middle is Darlington Hoopes, a Socialist who came to Reading when Mayor Stump came to power. Served as Stump's Assistant City solicitor, and ran for U.S. Vice President in 1944, and President in 1952 and 1956 on the Socialist ticket.

Supervisors, Leaders
City of Reading Playgrounds
1950

215

(previous page-)

Reading Playground leaders in 1950. Is your mom or dad in this picture? Are you? Third row second from right is my dad's cousin, the late Chet Druzba, who headed the Recreation Dept. for many years.

Mr. Druzba, whose nicknames included "Chick" and "Chubby", was credited for introducing something new to Berks County softball in 1936- the uniform! Dressed up players were said by the Reading Times to look like "a bunch of jockeys from Belmont race track." Chet was also the owner of Chet's Café in Reading, and served as manager of the very successful Druzba's Café Junior League baseball team in 1939, and was named one of the managers of the All Star game that year. On another occasion, the Times said, "We doubt if the City Junior League would be in its present shape without Chet Druzba, who manages Druzba's Café contenders. The pilot-pub man works hard to make the loop a success."

(Photo by John Tenschert, courtesy of Ruth Epler.)

Throughout the years, the aim of everyone, from the Pendora Playground Association, to many in city government had been not only to move Pendora up from the rat-infested mudhole it had been in the late 19-teens, but to make it a showplace- one of the finest parks in the city.

So when 1940 rolled around, the City decided to hold a special anniversary celebration- the 40th anniversary of municipal-owned playgrounds in Reading. And, after all the PWA-funded improvement projects that Pendora had benefited from, the City's choice of Pendora as the site of the celebration was no big surprise.

In a Reading Times article in late July, a week or so before the event, it was expected that the celebration would draw at least 2,000 people. Not quite a fourth of July crowd, but not bad. Part of the program for the celebration included a talk by a representative of the Olivet Boys Club. Funny how that name keeps coming up in regard to Pendora Park.

1950

1950 was, as the song goes, a very good year. Not just because I was born in 1950 ☺, but because the City Recreation Department and the Playgrounds were enjoying perhaps the peak of their popularity and prominence.

The picture two pages back from 1950 shows even more playground leaders than a subsequent picture from 1957. There was just so much energy in 1950 in the city playgrounds, including Pendora Park.

We know what sort of crowds that city playgrounds and parks draw today. If you see 1,000 on a given day, that's a big deal. But in 1950, the annual 4th of July celebration at Pendora Park drew 20,000 people! Those were the kind of crowds that Arrowsmith had drawn to the Pendora Amusement Park's opening in 1907, when the trolleys were still bringing people up from downtown Reading.

In 1950, the crowds still came from all over town, because the fireworks at Pendora were the best in town.

The picture below shows the crowd that kept the Pagoda Association's hot dog cookers busy that day.

Heather Boyer, who works for the Reading Recreation Commission, said she heard a rumor that the concrete stage had room <u>underneath it</u> for dressing rooms for performers. Could that be true? The answer at the end of the book.

4th of July, 1950 at Pendora. In the foreground, revelers stand on the mysterious concrete stage. (Reading Eagle)

Irma and Ruth Epler

East Reading Heroes

I first met Ruth Epler in mid July, 1998, when Reading was celebrating its 250th Anniversary. Ruth was a fireball then, a prominent member of the Pendora Park Association. She was listed as "historian" in the Association's commemorative handbook- a 20-page souvenir that I proudly took along with me after my few hours of volunteer work in Pendora's history exhibit on a warm July day.

That brochure included a small article by the late Robert Duddy, another influential Association member in the late 20th Century. Bob remembered the two elk (Buck and Kitty) in the zoo, the small softball diamond, and the large pavilion where the current basketball court is located... and how he used to play basketball under the pavilion, using the rafters as a basket!

I didn't see Ruth very much that day. Though in her 60's, she was everywhere, helping to make Pendora's festival a celebration to remember. The festival included a carnival, children's games, food vendors and bake stands, a petting zoo (without any bears named "Teddy"), a historical booth and tours, Hessian Camp re-enactors, a youth choir performance, Latin music by El Conjunto

Fantastico, Gospel music by the New Silvertones, a concert by the Ringgold Band (just like the old days in the bandshell), and even a reptile club exhibit.

None of these kinds of things would have ever happened at Pendora if it weren't for Ruth and the other dedicated members of the Association. They didn't just show up at meetings, they actually DID what needed to be done. She and Bob Duddy were confident about what was then the resurgent Pendora Park Association.

From the very first days of the big Fire at Pendora Park in 1911, there was an association of neighborhood activists who took it upon themselves to make Pendora Park a place where their kids could play and be safe.

Even in the days after the fire, when the park was a muddy mess, the people of East Reading banded together to make Pendora a place where their kids could play. The City never seemed to have money for anything. So when the park needed benches, the Association bought them. When repairs needed to be done, the Association got it done.

The same year as the fire, 1911, East Reading kids were treating Pendora as a city playground, and the City was noticing. Plans were made to purchase the park as a city playground. This was solidified in 1916 when the Egelman's Park lake overflowed.

When the City first purchased Pendora, in 1919, they still had the resources to get it fixed up. But money got tighter and tighter as the years went by, yet the work still needed to be done. And again, rather than wait for the City to do it, the Association did it. They would badger the City for new benches, lights, repairs, whatever the park needed. Most of the time, the City said "no money". So Ruth and the others did the work themselves. They staged fundraisers to pay for new benches. Pendora's sports field had the best lights in the City of Reading, and the Association paid for them.

In the 1950's and 60's, it was most likely my second cousin, Chet Druzba, who had to say "no" when the Pendora people came asking for help with the park. For a long time, when people would hear my name, they would always ask, "Are you any relation to Chet?" Now, it's getting harder to find people who remember him.

The Epler family had moved to East Reading in the late 30's from Stony Creek. When Ruth was just a kid, her mother Irma was the head of the Recreation Department's Costume Department. Yes, they actually maintained an extensive supply of costumes for playground events. And Ruth's mom

Irma made it all happen... creating bunny suits, and fixing Santa suits that the City rented. In the 1970's, the City sold off the costumes at auction, and some were bought by Meyer's Costume Shop in Temple.

Like her mom, Ruth never did it for the recognition, because there was seldom any of that. She did it because she really cared about the kids of East Reading- all of them- and she wanted them to have a nice place to play.

Whether it was selling hot dogs, or turning off the water in Pendora's wading pool every night in the summer, Ruth was there. (Ruth claims that at one point, she was the only one who knew how to turn off the wading pool water!)

She remembers when, as far as the Reading City Playground system was concerned, Pendora was actually TWO playgrounds. In those days, the upper playground was overseen by Kitty Kauffman, and the lower playground by Dr. and Mrs. Carabello. She remembers when all of the people in the neighborhood were members of the Playground Association.

Ruth became part of the association herself right after she finished college in the 1950's. (Unusual then for a woman). She remembers everyone working together to provide a safe place to play for all East Reading kids. She served as treasurer in the 1970's, and was always looking for things that the association could do. They purchased benches, put on Easter egg hunts, Christmas parties. And those dinosaurs behind the field house were Ruth's idea.

In the background, the back of the Field House in 2014, designed by Alexander Forbes Smith. In the foreground, one of the dinosaur playground figures- a testament to the efforts of Ruth Epler. (photo- Druzba)

In 1998, one of Ruth's Pendora chores was to turn the wading pool water on and off. Ruth says that, just a few years after that, the pipes under the wading pool broke, and it hasn't worked since. It's due to be replaced in 2016, about 80 years after it was first built. Not bad!

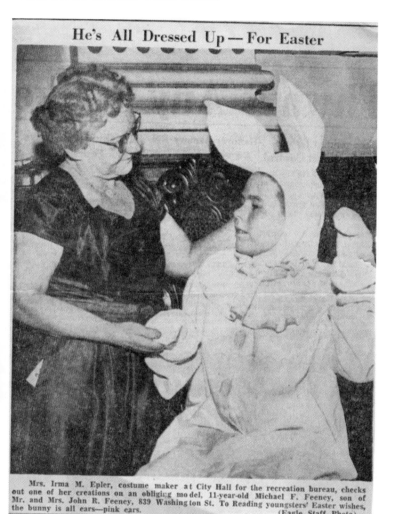

He's All Dressed Up — For Easter

Mrs. Irma M. Epler, costume maker at City Hall for the recreation bureau, checks out one of her creations on an obliging model, 11-year-old Michael F. Feeney, son of Mr. and Mrs. John R. Feeney, 839 Washington St. To Reading youngsters' Easter wishes, the bunny is all ears—pink ears.
(Eagle Staff Photo)

Do you know this boy? Irma Epler, left, shows off one of her Easter bunny outfits on 11 year old Michael F. Feeney, who can still be found hopping around in the city's Centre Park Area. (Reading Eagle)

The wading pool gathers leaves and weeds in the fall of 2014. The city is planning to replace the wading pool (sometimes called the spray pool) with a spray pad in 2016. An example of a spray pad being used in Connecticut can be seen below.

Ruth Epler has been living in the Pendora Park neighborhood for 75 years, and she has seen many changes. But it hasn't changed her feelings about the neighborhood kids needing a nice place to play.

What has changed is that Ruth is older now. In 2015, she's 81 (and a half!, she adds), and she doesn't get around like she used to. It's time someone else stepped in to fill her shoes. But that's getting harder and harder. "When I was younger, there were lots of people in the Association. But every year, the numbers went down. Now it's only a few."

There's not likely to be an infusion of financial help from the City for Pendora anytime soon. The City doesn't have much in the way of resources for things like Pendora Park. Of course, they've always said that.

In the meantime, the Pendora Park neighborhood shouldn't be waiting for miracles from the City. It seems that they could really use another Ruth Epler.

Then again, maybe it's just that times have changed. Today, people in a community are too busy to invest their time (and money) in their community, and they leave that sort of thing to government. If they had always thought that way, Pendora Park would never have been anything more than a swamp that became a housing development, like Carsonia Park. There's a good reason why, whenever someone heard about me writing a Pendora Park book, they'd say, "Talk to Ruth Epler".

Ruth Epler in 2015, after many years of selfless service to the kids of East Reading. On behalf of all the kids who play at Pendora, "Thanks, Ruth." (photo- Paul Druzba)

Back to the Future

I realize that I have only scratched the surface of the history of Pendora Park in East Reading. There's so much to talk about.

Pendora Park never got its swimming pool. Most other Reading parks didn't either. In the 21st Century, public swimming pools have become an expensive proposition. There again, pools are expensive for all the owners of backyard pools in the suburbs. The Socialists could have a field day with that statement, if they were still around.

Reading now has only one City-owned pool, at Schlegel Park. The pool that I learned to swim in, at 14½ Street above Cotton, is a private pool, and is still operating as of this writing, by the East Reading Swimming Assn.

In March of 2015, there was still a hurdle or two to be cleared before a new Olivet Boys and Girls Club could be built in Pendora Park, at the site of the old Miller's Family Park. The facility, 260 feet long by 64 feet wide, including the gymnasium, would be on the park side of 19th Street, facing Aulenbach's Cemetery, and displacing the large pavilion, which would need to be moved downhill a bit from its current site. The pavilion is worth moving, not only because it provides a good picnic spot for families, but also because it is occasionally rented out for events, and the city needs every dollar of revenue it can get. Despite an earlier plan to remove the beloved field house, public objection has insured that that won't happen.

It seems like poetic justice in a way to have Pendora host the Olivet Boys and Girls Club facility. From way back to the time just after the big fire at Pendora in 1911 and for many years afterwards, the Olivet Club repeatedly held fundraisers to help raise money for Pendora Park in general, and specifically for a pool. At least in theory, the idea behind all of the city playgrounds, including Pendora, has been to provide the kids of Reading with the best places possible to play. The new Olivet facility in Pendora fits right in with that theme. The following two pages show the floor plan and the elevation of the new Olivet Boys and Girls Club facility, as of March, 2015.

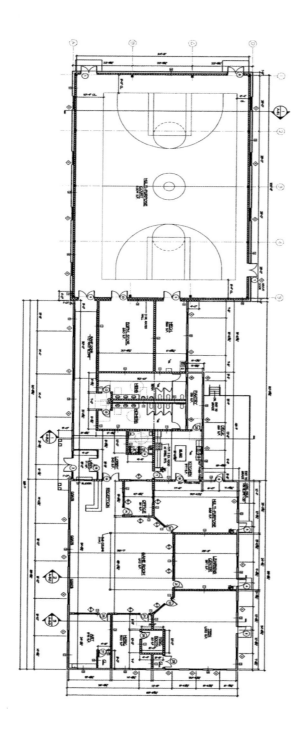

231

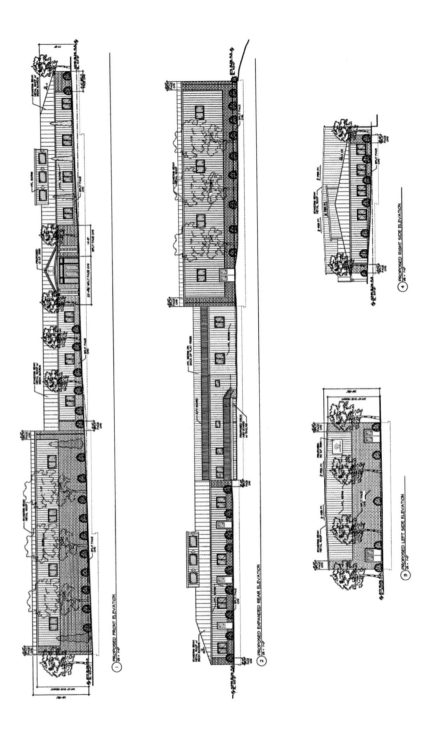

232

At this point, I think it would be interesting to look at another article from the Reading Eagle.

"A Pendora Park stream sent water rushing down 18th Street, where it turned the corner at Perkiomen Avenue and smashed into a corner house, then flooded 16th and Muhlenberg Streets, where cars were stranded in water that reached windshields. Perkiomen Avenue, between 16th and 18th Streets, had up to four feet of rushing water, which tore up large sections of asphalt. A firefighter walked into the flow of water rushing down Perkiomen Avenue at 18th Street, and was knocked down and swept for a block by the current. Several neighbors rushed to help him. Chunks of asphalt, some as large as five feet in diameter, were ripped from the street, causing rapid currents to form."

Sound like the flood of 1916? Actually, the article I just quoted was from September 8, 1987. I guess the point is that floods like this can occur at any time, and we must be prepared for what may seem unlikely right now.

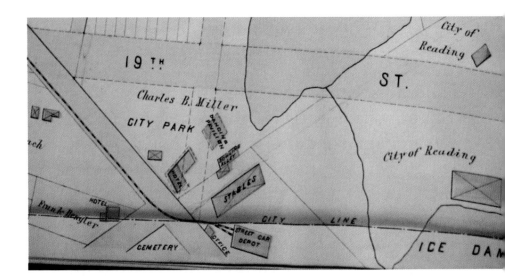

Map showing Miller's Family Park (called City Park) in 1884. The hotel was near where the large pavilion stood in 2015. Miller also owned a small part of the lake at center top, which was opened to the public in winter for ice skating. Also visible are the bowling alley and dancing pavilion (in yellow), as well as the trolley car depot and the stables for the horses which still powered the trolleys at that time. They would not be electrified for another four years. 19th Street, shown, only ever existed up to Forrest Street. Beyond there, it was just a paper street. So was Forrest Street beyond 19th, which is shown cutting through the hotel and the dancing pavilion. Site of the new Olivet Boys and Girls Club. (courtesy Sandy Stief)

In the process of writing this book, there were certain stories about the area that, although they were not directly related to Pendora Park, are still part of the story of East Reading, and help to give a sense of what life was like 100 years ago. Some of those were discussed at the beginning of the book.

Another was the following story from a place just across 19th Street from Miller's Family Park (and soon the Olivet facility), near Aulenbach's Cemetery.

This next mini-chapter is my way of saying thank you to my wife for her assistance with this book.

By the way, if I seemed harsh about the City government at certain parts of this book, I do not mean to generalize. The City has always meant well, and tried to make Pendora and all City parks the best they could be. They continue to do that now, as limited funds allow. As a whole, their intentions have always been noble. But over the years, a few of the city's civil servants have been less than noble. Again, same stuff, different year.

The Denglers & the Omega Club

On the extreme eastern end of what eventually adjoined Pendora Park was a hotel on Cemetery Avenue, on a small tract of land owned by Frank Dengler in the 1880's . Pay attention now, because this may get a bit confusing.

The Denglers are considered to be the founders of what became the borough of Mount Penn, the area called "Dengler's" before 1900. The family is a bit difficult to trace because of their insistence on using the same given names over and over again.

Historian Wayne E. Homan stated in a Sept. 5, 1971 Reading Eagle Sunday Magazine article, "When Mount Penn Was Denglers", that Dengler's Tavern, at 23rd and Perkiomen Avenue, which dated back to 1789, was purchased by "George Dengler" (no middle initial) from the Keehn family in 1840.

George (no middle initial) died in 1865, and the hotel property was passed along to his son, George F. Dengler. George F. owned the Dengler Hotel at 23rd Street until he passed it along to his son Charles in the 1880's. Charles also built the Glen Hotel on Neversink, and owned both until late into the 19th Century, when he sold the Glen hotel to- Newton Keehn! This is where my wife, who is a Dengler, comes into the story.

The original Dengler's Hotel at 23rd and Perkiomen in the 1890's, site of several banks until 2014, and then the current CVS Pharmacy. (Photo- Druzba)

According to Dengler family lore, George F. (for Frank) Dengler, my wife's great great uncle, did not get along very well with his brother, Frank Dengler. George F. had hired a substitute to serve for him in the Civil War while Frank had done his duty and enlisted, and the brothers owned competing hotel businesses around 1880, one at 23rd and Perkiomen, and the other on Cemetery Avenue, in Reading/Mount Penn. Oddly enough, the Frank

Dengler hotel building, which can be seen on the small map a few pages back, was about 95 percent in the City of Reading, and about five percent in Mount Penn. In the 21st Century, that could make getting a building permit a bit tricky.

Frank Dengler, who owned the hotel and property which became the Omega Club in September of 1893, had a son named George L. Dengler, (see what I mean about given names?), who had graduated from the Pennsylvania College of Pharmacy in Philadelphia, and was on his way to a successful career as a wholesale druggist. George L. lived at 22nd and Perkiomen, in the building that is now the Suburban Tavern. The building that still sits behind the tavern was where George L. used to compound his prescriptions. In those days, many of the drugs he prepared were made with opium, which was legal at the time. The prescriptions may not have cured what ailed you, but you wouldn't have cared if they didn't.

George L. was in his early twenties when, in 1893, he became a founding member of the Omega Club- a "reading and social club" in father Frank Dengler's old hotel. The library in the three-floor building eventually contained over 100 volumes, and the club was nicely appointed with very comfortable furniture. It would have served as a very pleasant "home away from home" for a young man, who would have relished a place where he could go to smoke cigars, drink a little whiskey, and talk to friends, while leaving his children with the missus.

This club was similar to the Wooden Ducks, except with a smaller emphasis on drinking.The Omega Club, initially limited to 14 members, had its own brass orchestra, glee club, and baseball team.

George Ludwig Dengler, founding member of the Omega Club. (from the family photos of Wanda (Eisenhard) Druzba, daughter of June Dengler, and granddaughter of George L.)

Eventually, club membership expanded, to the point of supporting TWO baseball teams. George L. Dengler was the right fielder on one of the teams. Although I obviously never saw him play, I do know one thing. He must have been pretty terrible. I know this because of George's position. I have a son who was a terrible baseball player in his youth, and they put him in... yes, right field, where I played for 12th and Chestnut playground, and where they put players who are content to "watch the daisies grow".

Omega Club members also enjoyed a two week camping trip every summer, and they had the club stocked with all the camping gear necessary, including two tents. The members eventually bought the building that they had been renting from Frank Dengler since the club's inception.

In the 1950's, the Omega club building fell on hard times. The Omega Club building was allowed to deteriorate. In the 1980's, the money in the Omega Club kitty that was left after paying off bills was distributed among remaining Omega club members- about 50 dollars each.

In January of 2007, the Victorian building which had been Frank Dengler's hotel, and then the Omega Club, was demolished.

The Omega Club building, just prior to its 2007 demolition. Pendora Park is to the right, and the boundary of Aulenbach Cemetery is just this side of the fence in the foreground. The street is Cemetery Lane. (Photo George M. Meiser IX/courtesy of Sandy Stief)

So How Big Is Pendora Anyway?

It would seem a pretty straightforward question on the surface. In 1909, when Arrowsmith's original land purchases were sold back to the Sweneys to satisfy the mortgages, the total area of Pendora Park covered about 8 ½ acres.

Through various land acquisitions, condemnations, etc., the park's area increased to 16 acres by 1929, according to several accounts. Since nothing has visibly changed at Pendora since then, you'd think it would still be 16 acres, right?

Wrong. In 2015, a check in the Park section of the City of Reading website showed about 6 ½ acres. What happened to the other ten acres?

According to David C. Ruyak, Operations Division Manager, Public Works, City of Reading, it depends on how you draw the lines between Pendora, Mineral Spring Park, and Egelman's. The truth is, nobody really knows exactly where Pendora ends, and Mineral Spring Park begins.

Ruyak said that Pendora's "deeded acreage" is 9.27 acres. And, between Mineral Spring Park and Egelman's, the total is about 91 acres. But exactly which acreage goes with which park is a matter for argument. Since the City owns all of the park land mentioned, they could pretty much draw the dividing lines anywhere they like. The postcard below is a good clue.

Reading, Pa. Mineral Spring Park.

This view from around 1900 shows some strollers (not the wheeled variety) at the southern entrance to Mineral Spring Park. Notice that the strolling path does not follow the Old Mineral Spring Road, which meanders off to the right, but rather adjoins Rose Creek, which flows on the left side of the picture.

In the background, one can see the Mineral Spring Hotel (now East Ends Athletic Club), and the entertainment facilities across the street from the hotel. The entrance shown is a few hundred yards up from the Lindberg Viaduct, the traditional limit of Pendora. But if you extend the boundaries of

Pendora up to the point on the postcard picture, you have well over ten acres.

Side Note- Farther up on the picture, just to the right of where the man and child are walking, is the approximate location of a plaque on stone, placed later to locate the Hessian camp, which was up the hill on the left of the picture. The plaque faces the path, the creek and the hill, where people would have seen it, and NOT facing the road at right, which is where we drive our cars today. So as you drive by, stop, get out, and go over and look on the OTHER side of the rock to see the plaque.

Let's get back to our acreage estimate.

With the land north of the Mineral Spring Park entrance added, it's now ten acres, right? Wrong.

A visit to Reading City Hall to see Andrew Miller of the City Planning Office, and Amy Johnson of Historic Preservation, was just in time. Due to the ongoing Olivet Boys and Girls Club project in Pendora, a survey of the park had just recently been done by John W. Hoffert of Shillington.

Hoffert was only asked to survey land up to the Viaduct, and the acreage that he came up with for Pendora Park was 12.93 acres. Again, that figure assumes that Pendora Park ends at the viaduct, and not at the southern entrance to Mineral Spring Park.

Figuring in maybe another five acres for that land between the viaduct and Mineral Spring Park, you have about 18 acres. And you also have to remember that some city land was absorbed by the Lindberg Viaduct project, including the house formerly occupied by zookeeper and gardener John Jacob Roth, which all would have made the 18 acre figure even larger.

By the way, if you stroll up into Mineral Spring Park, you'll notice that the pavilions look pretty spiffy these days. The City has been working on the park, and renovated some of the pavilions in 2014. They plan to continue the work, and make Mineral Spring Park more of a destination, as it was around 1900 in the postcard a few pages back.

The great stone work in Mineral Spring Park, though crumbling a little now, was another payoff of the PWA. If it hadn't been for those floods described earlier, that stone work might look a lot better today.

Gallery

I've collected many pictures and illustrations in my research of this book. Some of the unused pictures will appear in the slide show that I'll be doing on Pendora Park, similar to the one I do on Neversink Mountain.The following pages will also feature some of the pictures that I thought were interesting, but didn't seem to fit into the text of the story. Still, they're just too good to be left out.

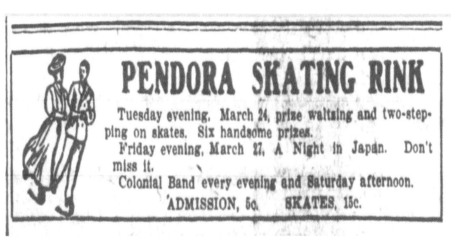

1908 Ad promoting year round skating. The admission charge was later dropped, but skates went up to 20 cents. In the end, 20 cents is 20 cents.

The Reading Traction Company car barn, near 19th and Forrest Streets, with the office on the right. (Foesig) Below-approximate location of the Car barn in 2015.

House at 19th and Forrest where a man was burned to death in a fire in 1945. (Reading Eagle)

Current site of Central Park, 18th Street side. (Photo-Paul Druzba)

Pendora Park Field house, with the concrete stage in the foreground. This is the same stage that appeared earlier in the scene from the 1950 4th of July celebration. Below- bridge over creek in lower park area. Beautiful, isn't it? (Photos- Paul Druzba)

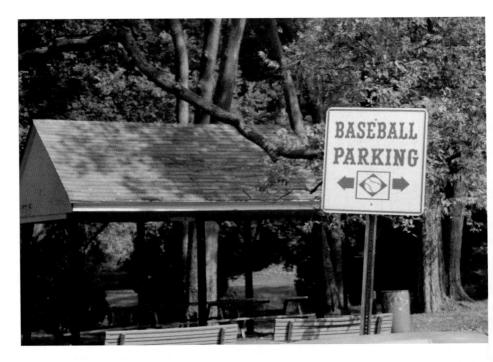

Above- pavilion in lower park area. Below- skateboard park in former tennis court area, near viaduct. (Photos- Paul Druzba)

Site of former Omega Club building, with Field House barely visible through the trees. 2014. (Paul Druzba)

Playground equipment in lower part of Pendora.

Vintage view of Rose Creek with Gravity Station in background. (Passing Scene)

Sandy Stief's mother Mabel at the Butt family house (the Pendora Cottage) in 1921. In the background right the original railing from the amusement park can be seen. (Sandy Stief)

Mabel in a winter scene at Pendora. Behind is the railing, and in the background, a park pavilion. @1925. The Butt family lived in "the cottage" until at least 1934. (Sandy Stief)

Beautiful steps and waterfall at upper end of Rose Creek, just below the former "duck pond" and tennis court and current skateboard park. Below- upper pavilion in 2014. (Paul Druzba)

Winter scene of the wading pool with the Lindberg Viaduct in the background. 2015. Below- duck pond, then tennis courts, now skateboard park. (Paul Druzba)

Closing session of the city recreation department playground leaders' institute will be held in the Pendora Park field house this morning, the playground season to open Monday morning and continue ten weeks. Attending the institute, covering nine days, were: Left to right, first row—Ruth Hauck, Mary Jane Rambo, Elsie Mae Wilson, Claude R. Buck, supervisor of maintenance; Earl Lorah, instructor in nature lore; Marion Shelmerdine, supervisor of girls' and women's activities; Thomas W. Lantz, superintendent of public playgrounds and recreation; Catherine Freehafer, supervisor of handicraft; Stewart Moyer, supervisor of men's and boys' activities; Anna K. Oslislo, supervisor of playgrounds; Miriam Klinger, Ruth Westley. Second row—Elizabeth Wagner, June Peiffer, Margaret Zartman, June Houck, Catherine Hannahoe, Jane Reed, Mary Kalina, Marjorie Solo, Esther Alpiner, Martha Ruth, Eleanor Heckman, Katharine Kaufmann, Mary Dunkleberger, Elizabeth Scholl, Mae Parker. Third row—Eugenia Moroszewicz, Beatrice Schilling, Emmeline Schilling, Evelyn Moyer, Ruth Shollenberger, Ann Bukowski, Mildred Trupp, Melba Kutz, Josephine Kercher, Gladis Fenstermacher, Jean Wetzel, Vera Kuhns, Mary Elizabeth Salzman, Agnes Graul, Edith Kuhns, Shirley Lengle. Fourth row—Eva Mae Lonaberger, Ralph Custer, Samuel Gundy, Robert Goldstan, Nicholas Fister, Marvin Angstadt, Carl Engle, Louis Rush, Aris Carpousis, Joseph Haage, Madge Arnold. Fifth row — Howard Hommas, Edward Winter, Chester Bright, Leroy Garrigan, Emerson Rothenberger, Daniel Breen, Theodore Templeton, John Tulley Randolph Mendelsohn. Playground leaders not in the picture—Frances Kintzer, Irwin Bright; supervisor of dramatics, Catherine Herb.—Photo by Tenschert.

Lined up in front of the newly opened Pendora Field House in 1939 are all but three of the city's playground leaders. Seated first row center is Thomas W. Lantz, the Superintendent of Public Playgrounds and Recreation. Get out your magnifying glass and see if your Mom or dad is here. Many city-wide playground celebrations were held at Pendora, which was seen as at least one of Reading's finest playgrounds. (Reading Times)

Folk Dancing at Pendora in 1930. Upper pavilion behind. (Below- Pendora's Dodge ball champs 1932. Both courtesy of Reading Recreation Commission)

Too cute to pass up. 1930. At the upper pavilion. As my mom would often say, "broke, but happy". (Reading Recreation Commission)

Pure joy at the wading pool. 1966. Note the Army helmet bucket. Photo by JR Cutler. Courtesy of Reading Recreation Commission

These kids were having a ball in the wading pool the year I was born, 1950. Courtesy Reading Recreation Commission.

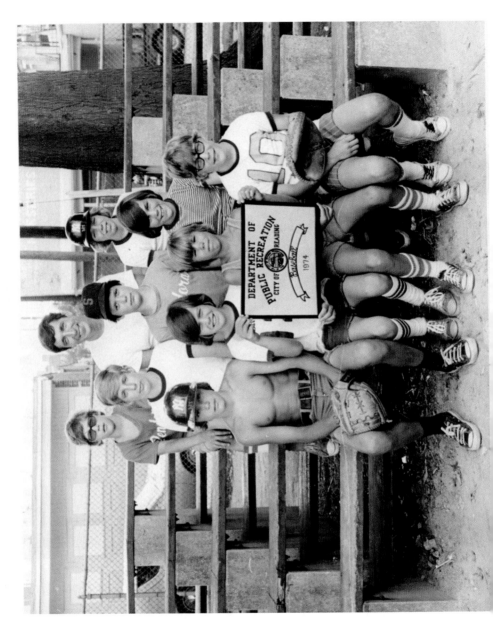

The Pendora Midget Baseball Team, 1974. These kids were playing ball while you were watching the Brady Bunch. Photo DJ Devine. Courtesy Reading Recreation Commission.

PWA crew turning the "lagoon" into a baseball field, 1934. Neversink Mountain in background. Empty far right peak of Neversink is where the Highland House had burned down four years before. (Note the abundance of small trucks and men, and the lack of power equipment.) (Reading Recreation Commission)

Top- Indian folk dance, 1976. 8ᵗʰ and Penn. Bottom- choosing sides for a baseball game, 1950. (Reading Recreation Commission.)

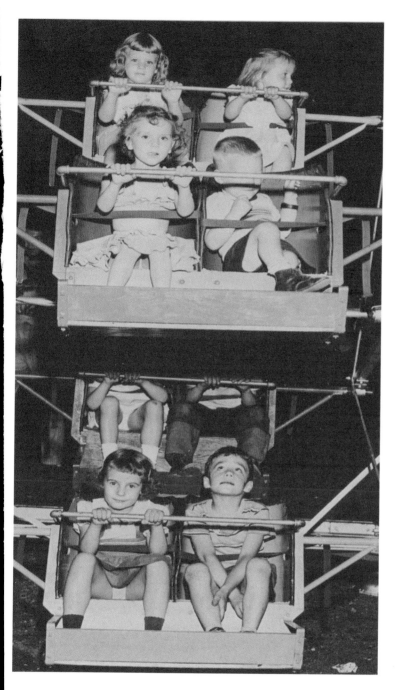

Fun on a ride at Pendora, 1950. Reading Recreation Commission

Mabel Butt, Sandy Stief's grandmother, in front of Pendora Park railing in 1920's. (Courtesy Sandy Stief)

This ad appeared in the Reading Times in August of 1897, advertising a Cannstatter Volkfest. Although it was only for two days, it did feature a "Magnificent Fruit Column"

Hockey one, hockey two… Box hockey at opening day at Pendora Park in 1955. The caption mentions Pendora as one of 42 play centers in the Reading area. I remember the hours I spent playing box hockey at 12th and Chestnut. I'll bet I'm not the only one. This photo was taken at the rear of the field house, on the lower playground when I was five years old, and I'm not one of the players. (Reading Eagle)

East Reading trolley car, early single truck model, at the intersection of 23rd and Perkiomen Avenue, around 1890. The gentleman near the front is my wife's other grandfather, George Hartman, who was the driver of the car. (Druzba/Dengler/Eisenhard collection)

Rose Creek flows down through Mineral Spring Park, and UNDER the dining room of the East Ends Athletic Club, Just uphill from Pendora Park. (Druzba photo)

Photo of a fawn at the zoo about 1920. In an adjacent cage in the background is the elk. Behind the elk can be seen the Rose Creek waterfall that descended from the duck pond. A last minute online purchase just before press time. (Druzba)

An early 1920's photo of the Egelman's lake, complete with swans, just uphill from Pendora and Mineral Spring Park. In the background is a Gravity Railroad car, stopping to pick up/drop off riders at Egelman's. (Druzba)